THE COMPLETE

ENCYCLOPEDIA

OF TEDDY BEARS

by Jacki Brooks

AN AUSTRALIAN DOLL DIGEST PUBLICATION.

Distributed by   Cumberland,
Maryland 21502

First published in Australia in 1990 by
AUSTRALIAN DOLL DIGEST
PO BOX 680
GOULBURN NSW 2580
AUSTRALIA

Copyright ©1990 Jacki Brooks.
Created, Designed, and Produced by M. A. Brooks and J. M. Brooks.
Edited and Indexed by Megan P. Bouris B. A. (Hons.) G.D.L.S.
Colour Separations by Prestige Plates, Marrickville, NSW, Australia.
Printed by Pirie Printers, Fyshwick, ACT, Australia.

AN AUSTRALIAN DOLL DIGEST PUBLICATION.

Distributed by Hobby House Press™ Cumberland, Maryland 21502

Exclusive North American Distributor
Hobby House Press, Inc.
Cumberland, MD 21502

ISBN   0 - 87588 - 365 - 6

PRINTED IN AUSTRALIA

TABLE OF CONTENTS

Acknowledgements

A book of this type could not have been completed without the help and encouragement of so many people. My heartfelt thanks in particular to my husband Mike, with him beside me all things are possible.

To all the Teddy Bear lovers who went out of their way to share their precious bears with me and to provide me with photographs and information. Their generosity, and support has been overwhelming. To friends and fellow bear lovers, David Worland, Angela Donovan, and Marjory Fainges, many thanks for their encouragement and co-operation.

To the companies that took the time and trouble to fulfil my requests for material, a big thank you. My sincere thanks and gratitude to the following companies and individuals for their assistance.

Photography and illustrations, when not otherwise marked, by Jacki Brooks, Teddy Bears from the Brooks Collection.

FRIENDS
Gerry Warlow, Bob White, Megan Bouris, Ross Schmidt, Gill Trotter, Anne Keane, Susan Weiser, Helen Jones, Nancy Finlayson, June Hayes, L. Albright, Robyn Cox, Obie Bronte, Debra Aldridge, Patricia Maiden, Wendy Benson, Myrtle Parker, Jenefer Warwick James, Nancye Aitken, Lesley Hurford, Jack Tempest, Ruth Floth, Faye Wiegard, Bradley Forgeard, Ray Horsey, Brian Hill, Dot Gillett, Christine Johnson, Janine Gibson and Pam Hebbs.

AUCTION HOUSES
Phillips Fine Art Auctioneers, UK; Mason Gray Strange Auctions, Sydney; Christie's Auctions, South Kensington; Sotheby's Auctions, London; Marvin Cohen Auctions, New Lebanon, New York State.

COMPANIES AND FIRMS
Australasian Sportsgoods And Toy Retailer; Pix; David Jones, Sydney ; Margarete Steiff GmbH; Angus and Robertson, Sydney; Anthony Horderns; Norman Lindsay's Estate; Grace Bros.; Jodius Pty. Ltd.; Doll and Toy Collection, Brisbane; NSW State Library; L. J. Sterne Doll Co.; Smithsonian Institute, Washington DC; Blue Shield Marketing Pty. Ltd.; Daily Express Newspaper, UK; Russ Berrie and Co. Aust. Pty. Ltd.; Gebr. Hermann K G; Metti, S.A.

Introduction

Collecting Teddy Bears is now an accepted and respected hobby. Auction houses cater to arctophiles, manufacturers and bear artists are busy filling our needs and books have been written on the subject - so many wonderful books.

So why another book on Teddy Bears? As the editor of the AUSTRALIAN DOLL DIGEST and a scribbler of articles on Teddy Bears, I so often have to refer to my library of Teddy Bear books and magazines to determine maker, age, etc. This can be a very time-consuming, albeit pleasurable, exercise and for a while I have thought how easy it would be if all these facts and figures could be compiled into one volume. Very ambitious? Yes, it is, and many times over the past two years I thought it couldn't be done. One tiny little entry could take hours and hours of research and all the hitherto recorded information on this particular subject could be contained in one or two lines.

Well it's finished - not complete, for new information about the wonderful early Teddy Bear makers is still coming to light and as this Encyclopedia goes to print no doubt it will have sections of it that will be out of date, but right now I believe this book to be the most complete record of facts and figures on Teddy Bears ever compiled. This doesn't mean that this book has made other Teddy books obsolete - the bigger one's library the better, either for pure enjoyment or to broaden one's knowledge. While this book contains pictures of hundreds of wonderful Teddies, they're not all pictured in here. My intention is for this book to be used as a reference book, an addendum to all other Teddy Bear Books. As a Teddy Bear lover, I never tire of looking at pictures of Teddies and I hope you will enjoy sharing the pictures of these bears.

A great deal of the information contained in this book has been compiled from books written by authors and researchers who have gone before. However, there is also a great deal of information that has not been published before. This mainly relates to the Australian history of bear making, but this does not mean the book has more 'Australian' content than say 'American' or 'German' content. It is a fact that the Australian Teddy Bear industry has never before been recorded and it deserves a place alongside the history of other countries' Teddy Bear makers. After the release of my last book, a pocket size edition price guide and identification aid, I was thrilled to hear from so many Teddy lovers from all over the world who had information to add to mine, or in some cases corrected my information. I do believe this is how we all learn and grow. The Teddy Bear world can only grow bigger and better from each published work and my hope is that each and every reader enjoys and grows in knowledge from reading this book.

ILLUS. 1. The cartoon drawn by Clifford Berryman for the Washington Post depicting President Theodore (Teddy) Roosevelt sparing the life of a bear cub while on a bear hunt in Mississippi.

The Beginning

Every Teddy Bear book starts in the same way with a short history on Teddy's beginning and by now I'm sure there are not many people and even fewer Teddy lovers that do not know this story. But it does have to be told for this is how Teddy Bears came to be.

There are three countries claiming to be the birthplace of Teddy Bears, although perhaps only two, the United States and Germany, are taken seriously. England, the third country, has never really put in a firm bid for the honour.

In the winter of 1902 the very popular President of the United States of America, Theodore Roosevelt, participated in a bear hunt in Mississippi. During the hunt a "black" bear-cub was left motherless and President Roosevelt decided the cub's life should not be ended. The famous cartoonist of the Washington Post, Clifford Berryman, immortalized the event with a cartoon captioned "Drawing the Line in Mississippi". Morris Michtom and his wife Rose owned and operated a toy and novelty shop in Brooklyn, New York. Inspired by the cartoon Mrs Michtom made a little bear and displayed it in the shop window. It proved a huge success. Mr Michtom wrote to the President requesting permission to call the bear "Teddy", the President's nickname. This was the beginning of one of America's largest toy manufacturers - the Ideal Novelty Toy Company, changed in 1938 to the Ideal Toy Company. Fact or legend, this story is the one most accepted as the story of the beginning of Teddy Bears. At about the same time in Giengen, Germany, a lady named Margarete Steiff was also manufacturing toy bears. These she made from sketches her nephew Richard made of bears at the local zoo. In 1903 these toy bears were displayed at the Leipzig Trade Fair. An American buyer was very impressed with what he saw and Steiff sold their first 3,000 bears. The order was increased to 12,000 by the end of the year and in 1907 the Steiff Company sold a record 1,000,000 toys. The history of the Steiff Company is well recorded and the consistent high quality and reliability of this company's product has made Steiff probably the finest toy manufacturer in the world.

The British claim to being Teddy's birthplace is a little hazy and stems from the then King Edward VII's nickname being "Teddy"!

No matter where their birthplace is, Teddy Bears are now made throughout the world and indeed have made this world a better place merely by being here.

Jointed Bears
(Teddy bears)

Ours articulés
(Ours Teddy)

a) slight manufacture
fabrication légère

size / grandeur, about/env. cm		21	25	27	30	32	35
pieceweight / poids par pièce „ „ gramm		0.65	115	125	155	175	210
Sealskin sealskin	No. III 126	⁒	⁒	⁒	⁒	⁒	⁒
Mohair plush, shorthaired Peluche mohair, à poils courts	No. II∅ 126	3.10	3.75	4.65	5.30	6.—	7.20

b) fine, strong manufacture
fabrication solide

size / grandeur, about/environ cm		20	25	30,6	35,6	40,6	45,6	50,6	55,6	60,6	70,6	90,6	100,6
piece weight / poids par pièce .. „ gramm		100	190	260	300	470	560	810	1.200	1,400	2,150	3000	4000
Sealskin sealskin	No.III125												
Mohair plush, shorthaired Peluche mohair, à poil court	No.II¢125	4.80	5.50	7.40	10.10	12.50	16.45	19.75	24.90	30.—	42.90	61.75	68.65
Mohair plush, longhaired Peluche mohair, à poil long	No.I∅M125	5.85	6.85	9.10	12.70	15.75	18.90	24.—	30.—	36.—	57.00	81.50	94.50

c) best, special manufacture, fine full form
fabrication spéciale de tout premier ordre

		shorthaired à poil court		longhaired — à poil long						
size / grandeur, about/environ cm		23	29,6 / 28	34,6	38,6	42,6	49,6	54,6	61,6	80,2
piece weight / poids par pièce „ „ gramm		125	220	330	480	590	750	930	1,500	2,600
Best soft Mohair plush Peluche mohair, 1ère qual.	No. Ia 125	7.40	9.95	15.45	18.90	24.—	30.90	39.50	49.75	92.7

ILLUS. 2. A page from an early Teddy Bear catalogue advertising several different types of Teddies in French and English. There is no cover to the catalogue and no maker's name on the pages, c1913.

ACRYLIC
A synthetic fabric used in the manufacture of modern Teddy Bears (see **Fabric**).

ADVERTISING
Many firms have used the Teddy Bear to decorate their products and to enhance their advertisements of products. Teddy has also been offered as

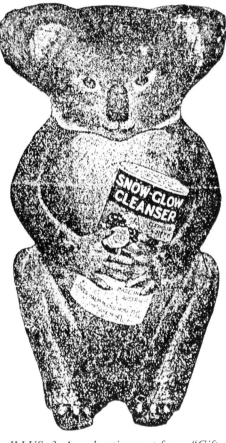

ILLUS. 3. An advertisement for a "Gift Calico Doll" from Every Lady's Journal September 1921 offering a 7in (43cm) high in five brilliant colours on stout calico - ready to cut out and stuff Koala type doll on receipt of part of the label of the Snow-Glow Cleanser label.

a bonus gift for the return of product labels box tops and the like. Some of the companies and products offering Teddy Bear give-aways have included:
Bear Brand Hosiery Co 1920s, Cut

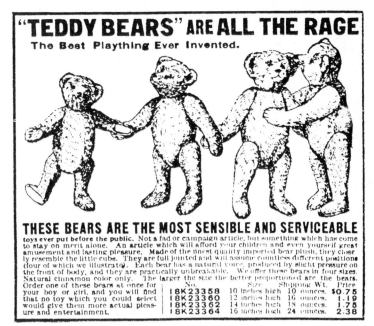

ILLUS. 4. A Sears Roebuck and Co. catalogue advertisement c1908.

and Sew, three bears.
Clairol 1958 Teddy with vinyl face.
Cuddly Fabric Softener 1980s Soft Teddy
Kelloggs Company 1920s Cut and Sew, Goldilocks and the three bears.
Lovable Bras 1975 Soft baby Teddy
Maxwell House Coffee 1971 Brown Teddy dressed in a red and white striped nightshirt and cap.
Snow-Glow Cleanser 1921 Cut and Sew Koala
Travelodge 1967 "Sleepy Bear" mascot, wears a nightshirt and cap.
During the latter part of the 1980s the number of companies using Teddy Bears as bonus gifts increased dramatically.
Such was the popularity of Teddy that his form could be found on all manner of things, including sewing and knitting patterns.
The Teddy Bear was advertised widely as "probably the most popular child's toy ever" and Christmas toy catalogues always carried a wonderful selection of Teddy Bears to choose from, all described in glowing terms including "The Best Playthings Ever Invented" - "practically indestructible" - "sensible and serviceable" - "soft and cuddly" - "made in golden Teddy Bear fur" - "Still the Favourite".

AEROLITE
(see **Chad Valley**)

AETNA
In 1906 G. Borgfeldt & Company were the sole agents selling the American made Aetna Bear. A fully jointed Teddy Bear made from the finest quality mohair. Made in seven sizes, the Aetna Bear was stamped "Aetna" on the foot.

ALOYSIUS
A wonderful old Teddy in the collection of the late Peter Bull, named Delicatessen (because he had spent nearly all of his early life on a grocery shop shelf) was chosen to appear in the British television series, "Brideshead Revisited". He was named Aloysius for his part and such was his success that the British toy-making firm of the House of Nisbet reproduced this Teddy in two sizes complete with scarf and British Airways

ILLUS. 5. A family of bears advertised in a Sears Roebuck catalogue c1908 priced at 25c "for the entire family". Note the term Teddy Bear is not used.

9

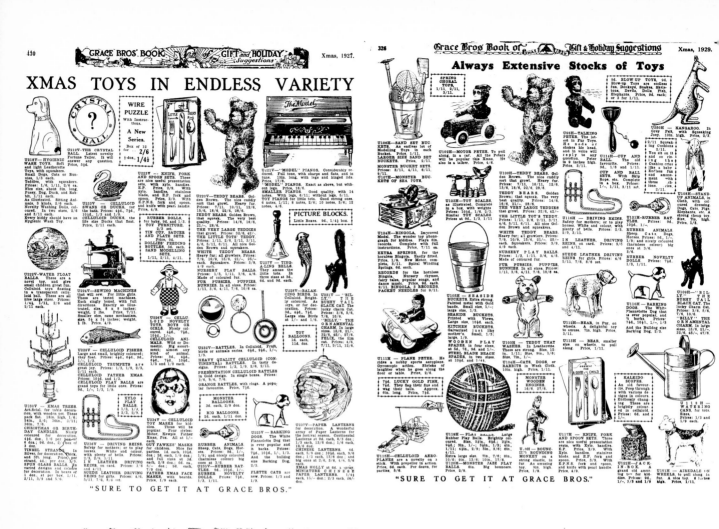

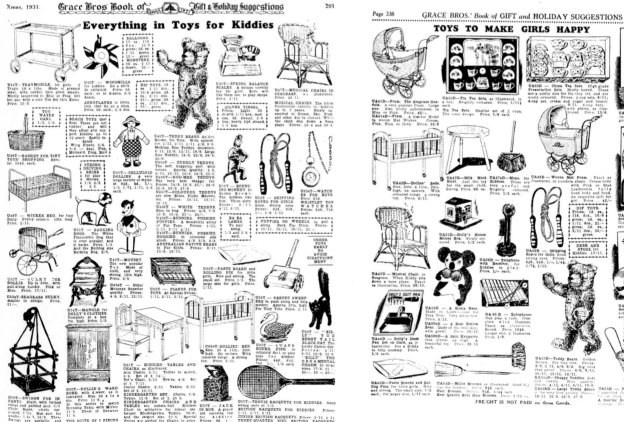

ILLUS. 6. Advertisements for the Grace Bros. department store for 1927, 1929, 1931 and 1933. Only the Teddy Bear remains the same for each year.

ILLUS. 7. English advertisement, October 1950.

bag. The reproduction Aloysius has all the patches, wear and repairs that Delicatessen has, all beautifully reproduced.

ALPHA FARNELL
(see **Farnell, J.K.**)

ILLUS. 8. Aloysius as reproduced by the House of Nisbet.

ALRESFORD
Makers of Teddy Bears and soft toys and dolls. Situated in Hampshire in the UK, this firm is well known for its beautiful quality dressed Teddies.

AMERICAN TEDDY BEARS
Teddy Bears have been manufactured in USA since 1903. The Ideal Novelty Toy Company (see **Ideal**) produced Teddies from 1903, along with other companies including:
American Doll and Toy Manufacturers
Art Novelty Company
Bruin Manufacturing Company (see **Bruin Manufacturing Company**)
Character Toy & Novelty Co (see **Character Doll and Novelty Company**)
Columbia Teddy Bear Manufacturer (creators of the Laughing Roosevelt Teddy Bear) (see **Columbia Teddy Bear Manufacturers**)
Eden Toys Inc (see **Eden Toys**)
Commonwealth Toy and Novelty Company (see **Commonwealth Toy and Novelty Company**)
Gund, Inc (see **Gund**)
Harman Manufacturing of New York
Hecla
Knickerbocker (**see Knickerbocker Toy Company**)
Strauss Manufacturing Company
Other American companies include:
Bearly There Company, makers of the Linda Spiegel Teddy Bear
Carrousel, makers of Teddies created by Doris and Terry Michaud
Gorham, makers of the Beverly Port Teddy Bears
North American Bear Company, makers of the Ted Menten creation, "Hug" as well as others.
Raikes, (see **Raikes, Robert**) makers of Teddies with carved wooden faces.
R. Dakin and Company (see **Dakin,R and Company**)
Stearnsy Bears
Xavier Roberts, creator of "Furskin" Bears (see **Furskin Bears**)
Many early American manufactured Teddies are unmarked, making identification difficult, American Teddy Bears do have several features that enable them to be identified as American made. Most are excelsior stuffed and quality mohair fabric was used on early Teddies. The overall shape of American-made Teddies appears slimmer than German or British-made Teddies with long thin limbs and little paw or foot shaping. The Teddies are fully jointed at neck, shoulders and hips

ILLUS. 9.14in (36cm) tall this early American Teddy is fully jointed, excelsior filled, shoe button eyes, old lettered sweater not original. Courtesy L. Albright.

and the ears do appear a little larger than German bears.

ANDY PANDY
(see **Storybook Bears**)

ANIMATED
(see **Novelty**)

ILLUS. 10. An early American Teddy Bear 18in(46cm) tall, shoe -button eyes, excelsior filled, fully jointed, unmarked. Courtesy L. Albright.

ANKER
A quality German made Teddy Bear with glass eyes, and jointed,which can be found with an open mouth. These Teddies carry a blue and gold

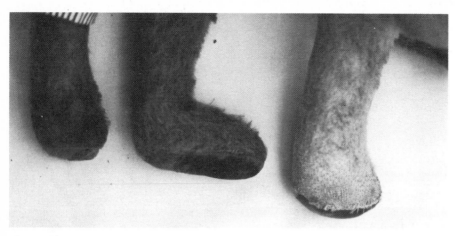

ILLUS. 11. These three ankles belong to Teddies of approximately the same size and age. (1) American made. (2) German made Steiff (3) French made, all c1920.

tag "Anker-Plüschtiere Aus München" on one side, and a lion and an anchor on the other side. Made during the 1960s.

ANKLES

Teddy Bear ankles differ in shape and can be used as an identification aid. Early American Teddy Bears have very little shaping to the ankles, while the German bears have very slim ankles that are in fact sometimes the first place to suffer damage as they appear almost too slim to support the beautiful big feet of the early German Teddies. British Teddies, made before 1920, also have slim ankles over large feet, however from the 1930s British-made Teddy Bears have fat ankles above fat stubby feet. Early French Teddy Bears have little shaping to the leg and the foot is not well defined.

APPLAUSE

A company owned by Larry Elins and Harris Toibb, who originally owned the distributing company of Wallace Berrie Company, which is now part of the Applause Division.

Probably best known for their product

ILLUS. 13. "Classic Teddy" from the Avanti range. Unjointed and soft filled.

Avanti a European-designed quality plush toy formerly manufactured under the "Jockline" label.

The Applause Teddy bears are soft filled, unjointed and of the highest quality with wonderful expressions. The "North American Brown Bear" and "Classic Teddy" designed by Jockline of Italy and manufactured in Korea are two of these Avanti Teddies. "After Eight" is an elegant bear in the Applause range.

ILLUS. 12. A "North American Brown Bear" from the Avanti range. Unjointed soft filled, made in a sitting position. The nose on this beautiful bear is soft vinyl.

ARCTOPHILE

A Teddy Bear lover or collector. From the Greek Arcto - Bear, Phile - to love.

ARMS

The shape of Teddy's arms can be used as an identification aid as the shape has changed over the years.

The very desirable early Steiff Teddy Bear, c1904 to 1914, has long, thin arms, looking quite out of proportion to the Teddy.

During the 1920s and 1930s the arm shape differed very little from maker to maker. The arm was plumper and looked more in proportion.

The 1940s and the 1950s saw the arms shorter. This was probably an economy measure. The British Teddy Bear was the most outstanding example of this with the arms being very thin and short in comparison with the body and legs.

Teddies made from the 1960s are more in proportion and the limbs are

ILLUS. 14. A Japanese made Teddy Bear with external joints. The arms are short and shapeless c1950.

not exaggerated.

Many Teddy Bears do suffer a unique condition of excessive wear to the left arm, due to being dragged about by a right-handed little owner.

ARTICULATED

To be joined together by joints that allow movement (see **Joints**).

ILLUS. 15. Alresford advertisement c1979. Courtesy Australasian Sportsgoods and Toy Retailer.

"BIMBO"
The Teddy Bear

4/11

10J14—Bimbo is 15in. high and made from fine fur fabric. He is an especially cuddlesome Teddy Bear. Price 4/11

David Jones 1936

F7138—**Teddy Bears.** Always a great favourite. Nothing to break. Made in Golden Teddy Bear Fur. 16in. Price .. .. **7/6** 20in. Price **9/11;** 22in. Price **12/11**

F7139— **Celluloid Dolls.** Heavy weight, new finish. Just like baby.

12in.	14in.	16in.	18in.	20in.	22in.
2/3	3/6	4/6	6/11	8/6	10/6

F7140—**Velvet Plush Golliwog** in colours. The **2/3** kiddies love them. Price .. ..

Marcus Clarks 1938

Left. "Teddy Bear of finest fur fabric. Moveable head, limbs, squeaks. 12in tall 31/-"
David Jones, 1952

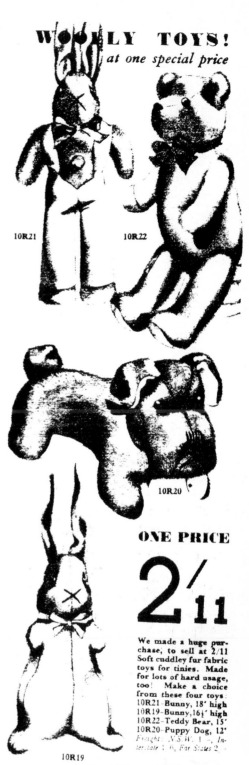

WOOLLY TOYS!
at one special price

10R21   10R22

10R20

10R19

ONE PRICE

2/11

We made a huge purchase, to sell at 2/11 Soft cuddly fur fabric toys for tinies. Made for lots of hard usage, too! Make a choice from these four toys:
10R21-Bunny, 18' high
10R19-Bunny, 16½' high
10R22-Teddy Bear, 15'
10R20-Puppy Dog, 12'
Freight : N.S.W. 1/-, Interstate 1/6, Far States 2/-

David Jones 1937

Golden Brown Colour

10R26—Still the favourite! Teddy Bear made of a soft, silky **9/6** material. 15 ins. high. At
Postage : N.S.W. 1/-. I'State 1/6.

David Jones 1933

ILLUS. 16. Taken from Australian Christmas catalogues.

13

ILLUS .17. The beautiful but worn Teddy is a c1907 Steiff. Note the very long arms, quite out of proportion.

ILLUS. 18. An Australian made Teddy c1930s. The arms are long and slim.

ILLUS. 19. A beautiful 1950 Steiff Teddy with short thick arms.

ILLUS. 20. A beautiful German made Teddy with frosted mohair and real leather paw pads. The arms are more in proportion. c1920.

ARTIST'S BEARS

This expression is usually used to describe Teddy Bears that have been designed and made by an individual and not by a large company in a factory situation.

AUSTRALIAN TEDDY BEARS

It is believed that the first commercially made Australian Teddy Bears were manufactured in Melbourne in the early 1920s by the Joy Toys Company (see **Joy Toys**); however as the Commonwealth of Australia's Patent Department has on record for

1916 an application lodged by one Charles Jensen for "Improvements in the Construction of toy animals - a toy bear", showing a method of attaching Teddy's limbs to his torso, production could have been earlier.

Teddy Bears were being advertised for sale from 1908. However these

ILLUS. 22. Mrs Dillman a migrant to Australia in 1954 embroiders a nose on one of the Teddies made in their primitive factory in a Sydney suburb. The brand name of Dillman products is not known. Courtesy Pix Magazine, c1955

Teddies could have been imports. Many firms were manufacturing Teddy Bears after World War II until the mass influx of cheap Korean and Taiwanese imports in the 1960s. This meant the end of most of the Teddy Bear manufacturing companies, as they could not compete.

Australian companies manufacturing during this period included:

Berlex (see **Berlex**)
Emil (see **Emil**)
Joy Toys (see **Joy Toys**)
Lindee (see **Lindee**)
Malrob (see **Malrob**)
Parker (see **Parker**)
Sterne (see **Humphrey B. Bear**)
Verna (see **Verna**)

The early Australian-made Teddy Bears were fully jointed, stuffed with excelsior, made from quality mohair fabric and with glass eyes (see **Eyes**),

ILLUS. 21. An English Teddy Bear c1950s Short little arms on a fat squat body is typical.

14

ILLUS. 23. A patent applied for in 1916 at the Commonwealth of Australia's Department of Patents for "Jointed toy animal having movable members jointed to the body member by means of opposing washers of different material held together by bolts and nuts substantially as herein described and illustrated in the drawing."

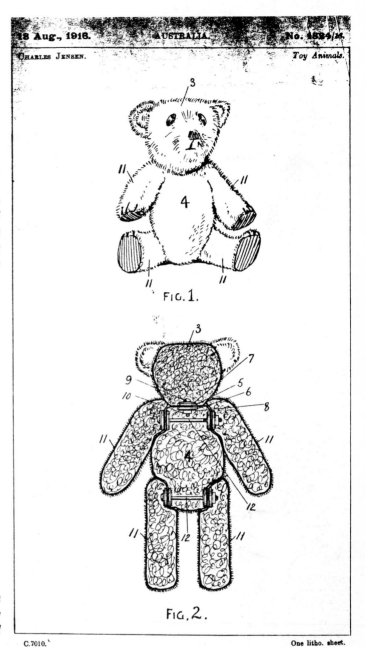

18 Aug., 1916.   AUSTRALIA.   No. 1524/16.

CHARLES JENSEN.   Toy Animals.

FIG. 1.

FIG. 2.

C. 7010.   One litho. sheet.

ILLUS. 24. A rare Australian made Teddy Bear made from kangaroo skin, with red leather paw pads. While most early koala bears were made from kangaroo skin it is very unusual to find a Teddy Bear made that way.

ILLUS. 25.
David Jones
Christmas 1914.

U 4242/4 — Teddy Bears, with movable joints, growlers, best quality. 5/3.

U/4242/5 — Teddy Bears, white, light brown, large size, 4/11.

LEFT
ILLUS. 26. Miniature Teddies designed and made by Australian bear artist Gerry Warlow.

15

1. Commander Grand Champion fur wire-haired terrier. From 9/6
2. Imported Golliwog with huge merry-go-round eyes. From 6/6
3. The Elizabethan, queen of dolls, exquisitely dressed. 8 gns.
4. A slightly older Dionne doll with real, curly hair. From 27/6
5. Clever English huntin' doll, pink coat, crop and all. 6 gns.
6. Rag nigger minstrel hectically clad. From 3/6
7. "Shirley" Temple in pleated organdi. From 25/6
8. "G-Man" Pursuit car with a flashing gun. 12/6
9. A quite life-like baby doll, soft body. From 25/-
10. Cuddlesome doll with go-to-sleep eyes. At 35/-
11. Soft, honey-coloured hygienic bear. From 10/6
12. Bright plush chicken wiv squeaker. From 7/6
13. Gay horse and cart that will separate. From 11/6
14. "Baby Betty" in hand-made clothes. From 19/6

From Farmer's Fairyland of Dolls

ILLUS. 27. A two page advertisement by Farmer's Stores of Sydney in their 1937 Christmas catalogue "Fashion Festival".

The Teddy Bear is advertised as "Soft honey - coloured hygienic bear. From 10/6."

17

ILLUS. 28. A rare 1908, 20in (51cm) black and white Teddy Bear by the Art Novelty Co. of USA.

ILLUS. 29. A bonus offer from the US food chain Wendy's Old Fashioned Hamburgers of a 7in (18cm) tall Dudley Furskin by Furskins TM bears.

ILLUS. 30. A lapel button advertising Bear Brand Hosiery Co. c1920

LEFT
ILLUS. 31. Mother Teddy, an early Australian Joy Toys is instructing the little girl in blue by the American bear artist Flore Emery to take baby for a walk. Baby is a fully jointed miniature by Australian Natalie Bergstrom. The tin plate pram and the kitchen dresser are antique.

ILLUS. 32. The boys in the workshop are both unmarked Teddies. On the left an Australian Lindee Teddy wears his checked
overalls and antique wool beret. His friend, an early American Ideal with very pronounced hump and shoe-button eyes in-
vestigates a tin of Bruin Paint by Baer Brothers of USA.

ILLUS. 33. These fully jointed mohair Teddies are by American
bear artist Barbara Sixby. Courtesy David Worland.

ILLUS. 34. These two Teddies are American made, both are fully jointed, excelsior filled with shoe-button eyes. The little fellow wears
a Roosevelt button printed in Newark, NJ, in 1896. The costumes are not original. Both bears made 1910-1920.

ILLUS. 35. Cowboy Bob by Bob's Bears Australian Bear maker, 18in (46 cm) tall, fully jointed with a shaved muzzle and moulded nose. Genuine leather hat and waist coat.

but very quickly Australian-made Teddies developed several unique characteristics that almost all of them share. They have unjointed heads and the front paws are usually slightly pointed and upturned. The Teddies made from the 1930s are flock or kapok filled with excelsior in the nose or sometimes the whole head and in the paws. Crumbed rubber was commonly used as filling from the 1950s. Paw pads on the earliest bears were felt. However oil-cloth or leatherette was usually used from the 1930s. Few Teddy Bears are manufactured in Australia now. Australian companies presently manufacturing quality Teddies include:
Buzz-Bee Bears

Grae-Waki (from New Zealand)
Jakas (see **Jakas**)
Gerry's Bears
Miffi Bears
Oz-Born Bears

AVANTI
(see **Applause**)

ILLUS. 36. Patterns for children's clothing in the English publication "Weldon's Home Dressmaker c1920."

B

BABY

A squat chubby Teddy Bear with rounded features is sometimes described as a baby bear. The youngest member of The Three Bears family is a baby (see **The Three Bears**). The German firm of Steiff produced a Teddy Bear called "Teddy Baby" (see **Teddy Baby**).

BALD

Usually the condition of a neglected or over-loved Teddy. However some "Bald" Teddies have been commercially manufactured from materials such as worsted wool and sail cloth, cloths that have never been "furry".

ILLUS. 37. A bald Teddy that never had fur. He is made of a heavy duty cotton (canvas) with real leather paw pads. A well made Teddy, the area where the head joins the shoulders is reinforced with leather. Fully jointed, 16in (41cm) tall with glass eyes, excelsior filled c1920.

BALOO THE BEAR

A bear character in Rudyard Kipling's "Jungle Book", in recent years brought to the screen by Walt Disney's film version by the same name. Steiff produced a soft toy Baloo standing 16in (41cm) tall made from dralon with a swivel head, the tag reads "W. Disney Prod. 0360.40/ Baloo".

BANDAGED BEAR

An unjointed soft filled Teddy Bear made from synthetic fabric. Sold by the Children's Hospital, Camperdown, Sydney, as a fund raiser. Each Teddy has a bandaged paw and foot from "falling off honeypots" and comes complete with his own adoption certificate.

ILLUS. 38. A working bear. More and more Teddies are being used by public services such as hospital and police to help children cope with times of crisis. This Teddy was made in Taiwan for the Children's Hospital, Camperdown, in Sydney.

BATTERY

Battery-driven Teddy Bears enjoyed great popularity during the 1950s and 1960s. The Japanese-made tin and fabric bears were produced well within everyone's price range. These animated bears have very complex actions. This, plus the fact that the tin parts of the toys are usually very well decorated, has made these toys very collectable on today's market. Condition and whether the box is still available determine the value of this type of battery-driven Teddy Bear.

Brand names include TM, Marx, Electro Toys, GBC, Linemar Co. However some of these toys are not marked or the brand name was placed on the cardboard box.

Batteries were also used in Teddy Bears to illuminate flashing eyes (see **Eyes**) (see **Electro**).

ILLUS. 39. Advertisement for Japanese made battery operated Teddies, from a 1956 Christmas catalogue. Courtesy David Jones, Sydney.

BEEFEATER

Beefeater Bear made by Merrythought of England (see **Merrythought**). 18in (45.7cm) tall, produced in 1973 and then again in 1988. The early Beefeater Bear has mohair head and front paws; the body, limbs and feet are "dressed" in the traditional Beefeater costume. The costume formed part of the body structure. The ears are higher on the head on the earlier Beefeater. The 1988 version has mohair feet as well as paws and head, and the head is jointed. Tagged to the foot and originally carrying a cardboard tag also, the 1973 tag is in the shape of a wishbone.

ILLUS. 40. Advertising lapel buttons. Courtesy David Worland.

TOP LEFT
ILLUS.41. A battery-operated Panda bear. He rocks, draws on his pipe which then lights up! The base and chair are tin, the panda is synthetic fur fabric over tin. Japanese made c1955. Courtesy Marjory Fainges.

LEFT
ILLUS. 42. A mint in box Japanese battery-operated Teddy. Made by Alps Toys-Tokyo-Japan and "R.V.T, a real value toy made by Iwaya Corporation", marked on the box, the Teddy is marked on the battery chamber "Made in Japan. R.V.T 3284 GYO". The Teddy is 11in (28cm) tall, made of synthetic plush with tin eyes, a hard plastic nose, the drum is plastic. c1954.

ILLUS. 43. Two beautiful big 28in (71cm) Berlex Teddy Bears from the 1940s. Both have jointed limbs, a stiff neck and are made from highest quality mohair. Note the bears have different types of eyes. The bear on the right has blown brown glass stick pin eyes, while the Teddy on the left has painted glass eyes and there is some paint loss from behind the eye.

ILLUS. 44. This wonderful hug of bears was bought at auction in London and is part of the original Peter Bull Collection. These Teddies now live in Australia. Courtesy Angela Donovan.

of Berlex Teddies are fully jointed, made from the finest quality mohair and excelsior stuffed. Very quickly the Berlex Teddies developed the stiff unjointed neck that is almost a trademark of Australian made Teddies. Kapok was then used as a filling. The paw pads are usually a cream-coloured vinyl. The eyes can be of the finest quality (see **Eyes**) or of the

ILLUS. 45. Beefeater Bears by Merrythought. The bear on the left is the 1973 version, the bear on the right is the 1988 version. The 1973 model still retains his original wishbone-shaped swing tag. Courtesy Marjory Fainges.

ILLUS. 47. The tag of a Berlex Teddy Bear. Red printing on white cloth tag that is bent double and sewn into the left arm seam. The tag reads "Berlex Melbourne".

BELLHOP BEAR

A term used to describe a Teddy Bear dressed as a bellhop with the costume incorporated into the body structure. The head and paws are gold mohair, the trousers are black and the jacket and pill-box hat red.

Schuco manufactured several versions of a Bellhop Bear from 1923, including a tumbling Teddy, a skating Teddy and a Yes/No Bear.

Bellhop monkeys were also made by Schuco. However the Bellhop Teddy is rarer.

BERG

An Austrian company, manufacturers of soft toys including quality jointed Teddy Bears. Made from the late 1940s, the Berg Teddy wears a red metal heart sewn to his chest, and a red rayon bow. The company's trademark is "Tiere Mit Herz" (animals with heart).

Early Berg Teddies can have a material label sewn into the seam of the left ear with "Berg" on one side and "Schutz" and the company's logo on the other.

BERLEX

Not a great deal of information is known of this Australian maker of quality soft toys and Teddies. Manufactured in Melbourne, Victoria, from the 1930s up until the great influx of cheap imports of the 1970s that put an end to many Australian toy firms as they could not compete with the cheaper prices. The early examples

clear glass painted type. The nose is black cotton thread sewn with vertical stitches. The mouth is of the same cotton and is in the shape of an inverted Y.

The Berlex Teddy is tagged to the right arm with a white rayon tag with "Berlex Melbourne" printed in red. The Teddies were made in several sizes. However I have not seen any under 10in (25cm).

The high quality of these Teddies was maintained until into the 1960s when synthetic fabric and soft filling replaced the mohair and kapok. The Teddies could be found both jointed

ILLUS. 46. A 3 1/2in (9cm) Schuco mechanical tumbling Bellhop Bear. His jacket is green, his pants are yellow and his bow tie is red. Courtesy Dot Gillett.

ILLUS. 48. The Berlex stand at the 1971 Toy Fair in Sydney. Courtesy Australasian Sportsgoods and Toy Retailer.

Berlex Soft Toys

ILLUS. 49. An advertisement for Berlex Soft Toys from the late 1960s. Courtesy Australasian Sportsgoods and Toy Retailer.

0251.34

ILLUS. 51. The Steiff 1988 Berlin Bear 12 1/2in (32cm) tall. Courtesy Steiff.

ILLUS. 50. A later 14in (36cm) Berlex from the 1960s. Jointed limbs, stiff neck, glass eyes and the distinctive vertically stitched nose and mouth. Paw pads are vinyl.

15/6

BILLIE BLUEGUM

10R33— The original Koala Bear. Made from blue Kangaroo skin. Rubber claws and nose. 13½ inches high. Priced at .15/6

Postage : N.S.W. 1/3, I'State 2/-.

10K31—"Billy Bluegum," the original Koala Bear. Delightful cuddle toy—made from finest blue kangaroo skin 13½ ins. **15/6** Post., N.S.W. 1/3, I.S. 2/-, F.S. 2/9

ILLUS. 54. Advertisement for Koala Bears described as Billy Blue Gum c1932. Courtesy David Jones.

KOALA BEARS
Wallaby skin, model noses, hands and feet.
P.Y.—5in. KOALA, 17/9. Post 9d.
P.Z.—6in. KOALA, 23/3. Post 1/5.
R.A.—8in. KOALA, 30/11. Post 1/10, 3/-.
R.B.—10in. KOALA, 41/9. Post 2/3, 3/8.
R.C.—12in. KOALA, 55/3. Post 2/11, 4/4.
Postage: 1st price N.S.W., 2nd Q. or V.

ILLUS. 52. Right. An advertisement for Blue Gum Babies c1956. Courtesy Anthony Horderns Stores.

ILLUS. 53. The 28in (71cm) 1940s Berlex Teddy showing his very chubby construction.

ILLUS. 55. A group of all-bisque Teddy Bears together with Goldilocks. Mother and Father are 3in (8cm) tall, baby is 2in (5cm), Goldilocks 2 1/2in (6.5cm) tall. All are marked "Germany", their clothes are original. They are seated on a Victorian shell decorated lounge. Courtesy Ross Schmidt.

ILLUS. 56. An illustration taken from an English children's book c1914.

ILLUS. 59. An early story book of "Rose Red and Snow White." This bear is definitely not a Teddy. Courtesy Marjory Fainges.

ILLUS. 57. An illustration showing a lovely big Teddy Bear. Taken from an English children's book c1910.

BOTTOM LEFT
ILLUS. 58. Blinky Bill by Anne Keane of Perth made under copyright. He has a porcelain head and feet with a soft torso and limbs. Courtesy Anne Keane.

ILLUS. 62. An English baby bowl decorated with Teddies running around the rim and signed by Jeanette Ruth. The bowl is part of the Teddy Ware range made by T. Lawrence (Longton) Ltd. of England. Measures 6in (15cm) across.

ILLUS. 60. A beautiful Steiff "centre seam" Teddy. Courtesy David Worland.

ILLUS. 61. A group of children's china, transfer decorated with Roosevelt Bears. All of these pieces are English made. The smaller cup and saucer are marked "H.Grindly and Co - England". The mug is marked "Empire Ware - Stoke on Trent - England". The cup, saucer and plate, "Paragon China - England". The Baby Plate - "W. and R. Stoke on Trent - Carlton Ware".

27

and unjointed. By 1971 Berlex Teddies shown in a trade magazine appear to be all unjointed. The early Berlex Teddy can be compared in quality to any made anywhere in the world.

BERLIN BEARS

The symbol of the German city of Berlin is a brown bear. Many German manufacturers of soft toys (including Steiff and Schuco) manufactured Berlin Bears to be sold as keepsakes to tourists to the city of Berlin. These Teddies are usually small, have a sash from the right shoulder to the hip bearing the printed word "Berlin" or "Grüss Aus Berlin" and wear a little gold crown.

As these tiny Berlin Teddy Bears were not made as toys most are of poor quality, and are unmarked.

ILLUS. 63. Two little Berlin Bears. The larger bear is 5in (13cm) tall and has jointed limbs. The smaller bear is 2 1/2 in (7cm) tall and is fully jointed. He wears his original BERLIN sash. Both c1950. Courtesy Ross Schmidt.

BERRYMAN, CLIFFORD K (1869-1949)

Clifford Kennedy Berryman is probably best remembered for his cartoon "Drawing the Line in Mississippi", which depicted the then President of the United States, Theodore Roosevelt, refusing to shoot a bear cub. From the cartoon and a New York toy maker (see **Ideal**) came the wide and wonderful world of the Teddy Bear.

However, Clifford Berryman was a well known political cartoonist respected by his contemporaries and peers long before Teddy lovers ever heard of him.

ILLUS. 64. A sketch of Clifford Berryman, by his son, J.T. Berryman. Courtesy Smithsonian Institute.

BILLIKEN

Made by E. I. Horsman of the United States, Billiken has a composition head on a jointed Teddy Bear

type body c1910 (see **Teddy Dolls**).

ILLUS. 66. Billy Blue Gum by Norman Lindsay, a suave and sophisticated worldly wise koala. The first character koala. Courtesy Norman Lindsay's Estate.

BILLY BLUE GUM

A character koala created by the great Australian artist and writer Norman Lindsay (1879-1969) on 11th August 1904 in the "Bulletin".

Unlike Blinky Bill, Billy Blue Gum is a suave and sophisticated politically wise grown koala. Norman Lindsay was a political cartoonist for the "Bulletin", a weekly, originally published by the Bulletin Newspaper Co Ltd, Sydney. During his long career, Norman Lindsay drew many koala characters, including the wonderful Bunyip Blue Gum in his children's book "The Magic Pudding". However Norman Lindsay's koalas were always

Left
ILLUS. 65. Billiken by E. I. Horsman. Fully jointed with a Teddy Bear fur fabric body and a composition head. This Billiken is 12in (31cm) tall, has a cloth label on his chest with "Y-O" printed on it. On the sole of his right foot is printed "Billiken" a drawing of a Billiken and "Trade Mark".

known as Billy Blue Gum even though the koala in "The Magic Pudding" is called Bunyip Blue Gum. Kangaroo-skin toy koalas were sold under the name of Billy Blue Gum during the 1930s. However the cute Blinky Bill Koala character has always been more popular and has been reproduced more often.

BING, GEBRUDER

A German company founded by brothers Ignaz and Adolph and in existence from 1856 until 1932. Firstly producing kitchenware and then in 1900 diversifying into soft toys. More famous for key-wind mechanical tin toys, this company produced mechanical Teddy Bears including walking, climbing and tumbling Teddies. However the company also produced non-mechanical Teddies. The Teddies are usually dressed and marked with a metal button, which can be fastened to the arm or the side of the torso or in the ear.
The button, marked "GBN" (Gebrüder Bing Nürnberg), was used until 1919. In 1920 the mark was changed to "BW" (Bing Werke).
The Bing Teddy Bears are of the finest quality, fully jointed, excelsior filled with either glass or shoe-button eyes.

ILLUS. 68. A Bing mechanical Teddy Bear c1910, fully jointed, shoe-button eyes, excelsior filled. Courtesy Phillips Fine Art Auctioneers, UK.

ILLUS. 67. A 11 1/2in (30cm) tall Gebrüder Bing Teddy Bear, shoe-button eyes, c1910. Tagged with the Bing button on the side. Courtesy Christie's Auctions London.

ILLUS. 70. 14in (36cm) cinnamon coloured Bing Teddy c1907 fully jointed, excelsior filled, shoe-button eyes. A metal button is fixed to the side of the bear. A bulky mechanism in the torso is inoperative. Courtesy Gill Trotter.

BISQUE

Hard porcelain fired with a matt finish. Several different types of tiny all-bisque Teddy Bears were manufactured in Germany in the years up to 1939. Usually unmarked except for the word Germany. These very collectable Teddies are usually in smaller sizes up to 4in (10cm) with painted features and the limbs usually wire jointed.

BLINKY BILL

This cute little Australian, now popular the world over, is a koala character created by Dorothy Wall, a writer of children's books.
Blinky Bill first appeared in 1938 in the children's story book "Blinky Bill, The Quaint Little Australian" written and illustrated by Dorothy Wall, published by Angus and Robertson Ltd, of Sydney. This book

ILLUS. 69. Blinky Bill created by Dorothy Wall, from the first book of the series "The Quaint Little Australian". Courtesy Angus and Robertson, Sydney.

was the first in a series as the cheeky little koala proved very popular with children. Kangaroo-skin toy koalas were made during the 1930s and sold as "Blinky Bill". However it was not until the 1970s that toys bearing a likeness to the drawn "Blinky Bill" were produced. The Blinky Bill books are now being reprinted and several excellent quality "Blinkies" are now on the market. These are made from more cuddly material than kangaroo skin and are soft filled.
A very popular Blinky Bill was re-

LIFELIKE animals on wheels . . . HUGMEE teddy bears and pandas . . . TWURLYTOY lambs and TING-A-LING rabbits . . . musical cats and miaowing kittens . . . puppets, poodles, shaggy dogs, . . . little pets for pram and playpen—the Chiltern 'Circus' is in town today. Beautifully made from fine quality plush, these cuddlesome animals are approved by the Royal Institute of Public Health and Hygiene.

See the Chiltern 'Circus' now — at Stores and Toyshops everywhere

Made in England by
H. G. STONE & CO. LTD., 31/35 WILSON STREET, LONDON, E.C.2.

ILLUS. 71. Chiltern advertisement, December 1956. Courtesy Woman's Journal.

ILLUS. 72. A 16in (41cm) Dean's Teddy Bear c1970s. Fully jointed, kapok filled, plastic eyes, velvet paw pads, no claws. This Teddy is tagged in his side seam with a cloth tag doubled over. The front of the tag reads "A Dean's Childsplay Babysafe Toy", the other side of the tag shows the famous dogs fighting over a cloth book, with the words "Made in Great Britain by Dean's Rag Book Company Ltd."

ILLUS. 73. A Teddy with a cloth tag "Made in England by Dean's Rag Book Company - London". 16in (41cm) tall, fully jointed, velvet paw pads, black claws, nose and mouth. His glass eyes are backed with a circle of felt. Kapok filled, long gold mohair c1938.

LLUS. 74. Three Dean's Golliwoggs. From left to right; 13in (31cm) tall printed cloth, on ... e bottom of the right foot "Mr Golly Dean's Rag Book Co Ltd London England" and on ... e left foot, the picture of the two fighting dogs together with "Trade mark Registered in ... ll Countries" c1960s. Centre, 20in (70cm) tall, all felt with celluloid eyes and a sheepskin ... ig. Tagged to the right foot "Made in England by Dean's Rag Book Co Ltd LONDON." ... 1920s. Right 14in (35cm) tall printed cloth with a felt jacket. Plastic clip-in eyes. Tagged ... the centre back seam with a printed cloth tag "Dean's Childsplay Toys Ltd. Rye, Sussex. ... onforms to British Standards BS 3443 U.S.A. Reg No PA 180 and MASS 181, Manufac- ... ed in all "New Materials" Made in England" c1950s.

ILLUS. 75. An early Dean's Teddy Bear c1912. Gold mohair, glass eyes, fully jointed, kapok filled. Claws and nose and mouth embroidered in black. Replaced paw pads.

31

ILLUS. 76. A beautiful Blinky Bill, 18in (46cm) tall, tagged. "Copyright Angus and Robertson", "The Famous Australian Blinky Bill Character. Bomba Pty Ltd, made in Australia from genuine Australian Sheepskin". Blinky has large plastic eyes and nose and is unjointed. Courtesy Marjory Fainges.

leased recently made by Bomba Pty Ltd of Australia, tagged "Copyright Angus and Robertson. The famous Australian Blinky Bill Character. Bomba Pty Ltd, made in Australia from genuine Australian Sheepskin". He is 18in (46cm) tall and wears a pair of blue cotton pants and a blue bow. Another quality Blinky on the market is by Australian doll artist Anne Keane of Western Australia. Anne's Blinky is made under copyright, he has porcelain head and feet with a soft torso and limbs, he wears checked overalls and black boots.

BOBBY BEAR
(See **Storybook Bears**)

BOOK ILLUSTRATIONS
Teddy's popularity has made him a prime subject to illustrate children's books, not as the hero (see **Storybook Bears**) but as merely a decoration. Hardly a children's picture book has been printed that does not contain pictures of the versatile Teddy Bear.

BOSTON, WENDY
An English doll and toymaker since 1955. Teddy Bears, soft toys and dolls were sold under the name of

ILLUS. 77. Wendy Boston Teddy Bear advertised in 1959. Courtesy Grace Bros.

"Playsafe". By 1956 the firm had undergone a name change to "Wendy Playsafe Toys Ltd". These toys, including the Teddy Bears, were filled with machine-washable plastic sponge. Wendy Boston Teddies are unjointed and fitted with "safe" plastic eyes. The firm was taken over in 1968 by Denys Fisher Toys Ltd, but still retained the name Wendy Boston.

ILLUS. 78. A Wendy Boston Playsafe Teddy, 20in (51cm) tall, unjointed, filled with machine-washable filling.

ILLUS. 80. A rare porcelain china Blinky Bill. A faithful copy of the Dorothy Wall character. He has a hole moulded into his right hand, perhaps to carry a flag or a fishing pole. Unsigned 6in (15cm) tall c1930s.

BOTTLES
Several different companies have made bottles in the shape of Teddy Bears to hold their products. Probably the most well known is by the cosmetic company Avon who released a clear glass bottle with a gold head and later a flocked glass bottle, both in the shape of a Teddy.

The firm of Schuco (see **Novelty**) produced a wonderful perfume bottle disguised as a Teddy Bear.

ILLUS. 79. Wendy Boston display stands at the Sydney Toy Trade Fairs in 1970 and 1971. Courtesy Australasian Sportsgoods and Toy Retailer.

ILLUS. 81. A rare rubber hot water bottle in the shape of a koala c1930s. Very well detailed, the neck is marked "Koala Made in Australia"

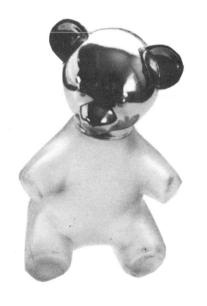

ILLUS. 83. A Teddy Bear bottle by Avon Cosmetics c1970s. A label on the base of the bottle reads "Avon Teddy Bear Decanter, Pretty Peach. Avon Products Pty Ltd, Sydney 20ml".

BRUIN BEARS
As distinct from Teddy Bears. Toy life-like bears made before the arrival of Teddy. Can also refer to realistic looking bears found on clocks, ornaments, etc.

ILLUS. 82. A typical pre Teddy, Victorian bear. A scrap pasted into a book c1898.

BRUIN BEARS
A line of Teddies made by Chiltern of England (see **Chiltern**).

BRUIN MANUFACTURING COMPANY
Manufacturers of quality Teddy Bears in the first quarter of this century in New York. These rare Teddies are fully jointed, made from quality mohair, shoe-button eyes and excelsior stuffed. Originally tagged to the foot "BMC".

BULL, PETER
Usually accepted as the "Father" of the modern Teddy Bear revival.
In the late 1960s the now deceased Mr Peter Bull placed an advertisement in "The Times" newspaper, "History of E Bear, Esquire, Reminiscences, Data, Photographs (returnable) urgently requested by Peter Bull, who is compiling a symposium on these remarkable creatures".
Peter Bull wrote "The Teddy Bear Book" and over the years acquired many Teddy Bears in his unasked for collection. He always insisted he was

not a collector, "merely an arctophile" (a lover of bears).
Delicatessen (see **Aloysius**), the star of the television series "Brideshead Revisited", was from Peter Bull's collection.
The House of Nisbet created Bully Bears (see **Bully Bears**) in collaboration with Peter.
After his death in May 1984 his collection was passed on to the Toy and Model Museum in London, England. However part of the collection was bought at a doll and toy auction in London and brought to live in Australia.

ILLUS. 84. The late Peter Bull with his namesake Bully Bear by the House of Nisbet. Courtesy Australasian Sportsgoods and Toy Retailer.

ILLUS. 85. A "Bully Bear" made exclusively for the London store of Harrods. Courtesy Australasian Sportsgoods and Toy Retailer.

33

ILLUS. 86. Peter Bull together with Aloysius, Bully Bear and Bully Bear Jnr. This picture was used on the back of the presentation case of "The Teddy Bear Book" by Peter Bull, published by House of Nisbet. Courtesy Australasian Sportsgoods and Toy Retailer.

BULLY BEARS
The name of a range of Teddy Bears made by the House of Nisbet Ltd of England in 1981.

Made of quality mohair, fully jointed and sporting a long nose and a hump, these Teddies were created by the House of Nisbet with the close collaboration of Peter Bull.

Other Teddies in this series include Bully Minor, Young Bully and Captain Bully.

BURBANK TOYS
(See **Rupert Bear**)

BUTTONS
Several manufacturers of Teddy Bears use a metal button attached to the Teddy as a means of identification.

The most well known is of course the German firm of Steiff (see **Steiff**) which uses a metal button affixed to a Teddy's ear and actually uses the term "Button in the ear" (Knopf Im Ohr) as its trademark. With the exception of the very earliest applied buttons, which are blank, the word Steiff is pressed into the metal. The markings on the buttons can not be used to help determine the age of a Steiff Teddy as in time of shortage within the Steiff factory old buttons were used. A Steiff Teddy that has lost his button for one reason or another is usually valued at less than a similar Teddy that still retains his.

The English toy making company of Merrythought (see **Merrythought**) also used a metal button affixed to

Teddy's ear as a means of identification. This was done for a very short time in the early years of production, in the 1930s. The button used by Merrythought is metal covered with celluloid and bears the company's trademark of a wishbone and "Hygienic Merrythought Toy Made in England Regd. Trade Mark". Often this celluloid covering is missing, leaving just a blank metal button.

Another English firm to use a metal button as a means of identification was Chad Valley (see **Chad Valley**). These bears carried a metal button covered with celluloid which bore the wording "Chad Valley British Hygienic Toys". However the Chad Valley button was not always affixed to the ear. It was sometimes placed on parts of Teddy's torso. As with the Merrythought button the Chad Valley button can have lost its celluloid cover over the years.

Bing Teddy Bears (See **Bing, Gebrüder**) carried a metal tag bearing the company's initials.

During the early 1900s Teddy Bears were used to decorate clothing buttons. These are now considered highly collectable by both button collectors and arctophiles alike.

ILLUS. 87. Brass Teddy Bear buttons, c1907. Courtesy David Worland.

CANTERBURY BEARS

An English firm established as a family concern in 1979. Production commenced in 1980, and in January 1981 the Teddies were exhibited for the first time at the Earls Court Toy Fair in London. The firm has gone from strength to strength manufacturing modern and traditional quality Teddy Bears.

ILLUS. 89. An early Canterbury Bear from 1982.Courtesy Australasian Sportsgoods and Toy Retailer.

ILLUS. 88. Celluloid Teddy Bears 5in (13cm) tall, jointed limbs. Made in Japan, the centre bear is marked on the foot Made in Japan. c1940s. Courtesy Ross Schmidt.

CELLULOID

Several types of celluloid Teddy Bears were produced by Japanese firms during the 1930s and '40s. Usually made in very bright colours such as hot pink, red and blue etc. Some with moulded neck frills and bows. These Teddies are jointed at the shoulders and hips with fixed heads. They are always in the smaller sizes of up to 5in (13cm).Usually unmarked.However some are marked with a fleur de lis and "Made in Japan".

CENTRE SEAM BEARS

A term used to describe a Steiff Teddy Bear with a seam running down the centre of the head between the ears to the nose. These bears are very desirable to collectors, and were thought to be a special rare style. The real reason for Centre Seam Teddies is much simpler; Steiff's explanation follows:

"Steiff were able to cut six normal Teddy Bear heads from each length of Mohair, but their template was too large to make a seventh head. In order to avoid unnecessary wastage Steiff cut two halves from the seventh template and therefore some bears are found with a centre-seam."

CHAD VALLEY

An English company, founded in 1823 by Anthony Bunn-Johnson as printers and bookbinders in Birmingham. The company moved premises in 1897 to a larger factory beside the river Chad.

In 1919 the Johnson family saw an opportunity to expand the business to include the manufacture of dolls, soft toys, board games and jigsaw puzzles as the importation of this type of goods from Germany had been banned during World War I. The name Chad Valley was taken at this time.

In 1920 the company was manufacturing Teddy Bears. The range was wide and varied including a brightly coloured mohair Teddy (considered very rare). The larger bears were fitted with the "Patent

ILLUS. 90. Canterbury Bear Family from 6in (15cm) to 27in (69cm) featuring safety lock eyes, suede or leather paws, fully jointed with wooden discs c1985. Courtesy Jodius Pty Ltd.

ILLUS. 91. The cover of the English trade journal "Games and Toys", October 1950 featuring Chad Valley Teddy Bears and Soft Toys.

land by Chad Valley". In 1938 The Chad Valley Company was appointed as toymaker to Her Majesty the Queen. The label then changed to a larger square shape and included a picture of the royal coat of arms together with "The Chad Valley Co Ltd by Appointment Toymaker to H M Queen Elizabeth, the Queen Mother". The beautiful quality of the Chad Valley Teddy makes it a firm favourite with collectors. A fully jointed Teddy, with kapok stuffing, one of the characteristics of a Chad Valley Teddy is his large nose.

RIGHT
ILLUS. 94. An early 18in (46cm) tall Chad Valley Teddy c1920s. Fully jointed, glass eyes. This charming old Teddy has a button in his right ear that reads "Chad Valley - Aerolite - Trade Mark". Courtesy Doll and Toy Collection, Brisbane.

Chad Valley Growler". The Chad Valley Teddy came in thirteen different sizes and six qualities of fabric. The very earliest Chad Valley bears were buttoned (see **Buttons**), then up until 1938 an oblong shape cloth tag was sewn to the foot of the bear stating "Hygienic Toys - Made in England by Chad Valley".

ILLUS. 92. Chad Valley cloth tags, the square one from after 1938 the oblong one from before.

ILLUS. 93. A close-up of the early Chad Valley button c1920s "Chad Valley - Aerolite - Trade Mark." Courtesy Doll and Toy Collection, Brisbane.

ILLUS. 95. Two Teddies and a rare cloth baby doll all tagged Chad Valley. The doll is tagged on both feet "The Chad Valley Co Pty Ltd - By Appointment Toymakers to H M the Queen" a square tag on the left foot and "Hygienic Toys Made in England by Chad Valley" an oblong tag on the right. This doll has both the tag before 1938 and the tag after 1938. The Teddies are tagged "The Chad Valley Co Ltd - By Appointment - Toymaker to Queen Elizabeth the Queen Mother" on a square cloth tag.

CHARACTER TEDDY BEARS

Teddy Bears known by name and appearing in story books, films, television etc, are known as Character Bears and include such famous individual Teddies as

Aloysius (see **Aloysius**)

Billy Blue Gum (see **Koala Bear and Billy Blue Gum**)

Blinky Bill (**see Blinky Bill**)

Humphrey B. Bear (see **Humphrey B. Bear**)

Misha (see **Misha**)

Paddington (see **Paddington**)

Rupert (see **Rupert Bear**)

Winnie the Pooh (see **Winnie the Pooh**)

CHARACTER TOY AND NOVELTY COMPANY

An American manufacturer of Teddy Bears, whose early Teddies were fully jointed with glass eyes. These quality Teddies were manufactured from 1920. Tagged to the ear with a cloth tag, the tag reads "Character, Designed by Character Novelty Co Inc, So Norwalk, Conn."

Later Teddies were unjointed and soft filled, they also carried a cardboard label. Teddy Bears made by this company during the 1930s can have a metal nose.

ILLUS. 96. 12in (31cm) gold mohair fully jointed Teddy by Character Toy and Novelty Co. This Teddy Bear has shoe-button eyes and felt paw pads. Tagged in the ear "Character" c1940. Courtesy Susan Weiser.

RIGHT
ILLUS. 97. Two Character Toy and Novelty Co bears. The larger Teddy 12in (31cm) on the left is unjointed, light brown mohair with shoe button eyes over round pieces of felt - a characteristic of this firm. The standing Teddy is 7in (18cm) tall and has the remnants of a red felt tongue. Both bears unmarked c1950s. Courtesy Susan Weiser.

CHASSIS TOYS

A manufacturer's term for toys attached to a wheeled chassis. (see **Wheels**)

CHEEKY

First produced in 1957 and still in

ILLUS. 98. A beautiful example of a 1950s Merrythought Cheeky. 13in (33cm) tall made from gold mohair with brown round felt front paw pads and tan paw pads on his feet. He has the large black wrap-around claws favoured by the Merrythought Company, a velvet muzzle and bells in his ears. He wears a satin quilted embroidered baby bib.

production. A style of Teddy made by Merrythought of England (see **Merrythought**). A round face, smiling baby bear with ears on the side of the

head. Can be made from mohair or art silk plush and "Cheeky" can have bells in the ears. Tagged to the right foot with cloth tag, "Merrythought-Ironbridge-Shrops Made in England". Also cardboard label sewn on the chest. The label is in the shape of a Wishbone and reads "Merrythought - Hygienic Toys - Made in England".

CHILTERN

An English firm which first used the name Chiltern in 1921. A partnership between H. G. Stone (also a partner of the Farnell Toy Company) and L. Reese, the firm produced soft toys and dolls from 1920. The company was located in London and was well known for its quality products. During the 1940s the firm advertised their Teddy Bears as "Hugme" bears while other soft toys were referred to as "Chiltern". The "Hugme" bears are fully jointed, kapok filled and made from gold mohair. They have a cloth tag on the side seam stating "Chiltern

ILLUS.99. A 15in (38cm) Merrythought Cheeky made from Art Silk plush, the colour is slightly variegated. The paw pads are brown felt with wraparound claws tagged to the right foot "Merrythought, Ironbridge, Shrops. Made in England, Regd. Design". A velvet muzzle with a smiling baby face and bells in the low set ears make Cheeky a firm favourite with collectors.

ILLUS. 100. A beautiful big boy bear. A 36in (91cm) Chiltern Teddy Bear c1950. Fully jointed and made from quality mohair. The head is excelsior filled, the body and limbs are filled with kapok. Teddies of this size are rare. Courtesy Helen Jones.

ILLUS. 101. A fully marked mint condition Chiltern bear of the 1950s. Bought from a closed toy store. 11in (38cm) tall the bear wears a cardboard swing tag sewn on to the chest "Made in England, Chiltern Toys. Awarded the Certificate of the Institute of Hygiene" and on the other "Trade Mark, Chiltern Toys, Made in England". A cloth tag stuck on the right foot paw pad reads "Chiltern Toys Made in England". This fully jointed little Teddy shows a definite decline in quality from earlier Chiltern Teddy Bears.

ILLUS. 102. A 14in (36cm) tall Chiltern Teddy with a moulded rubber nose, fully jointed, kapok filled leatherette paw pads. His wooden bead necklace has been with him for a long time.

ILLUS. 100.

ILLUS. 101.

ILLUS. 103. A beautiful big 28in (71cm) Chiltern Teddy Bear. He has a tag in his head seam at the neck edge almost hidden. Fabulous dense mohair, leatherette paw pads and a moulded nose. A typical chubby English Teddy of the 1940s-50s period.

ILLUS. 104. This sweet little Teddy Bear is 12in (31cm) tall, fully jointed with velvet paw pads. Very long mohair, light brown in colour. An exceptional quality Chiltern Teddy Bear of the 1930s in near mint condition with loads of appeal.

ILLUS. 102.

ILLUS. 103.

ILLUS. 104.

Hygienic Toys made in England". One version of the "Hugme", a 17in (43cm) Teddy came fitted with a Swiss music box.

"Bruin Bears" were also advertised in 1950. They were made in four sizes and fitted with a "Ting-a-ling", a tinkling device operated when Teddy was tipped up. A "Ting-a-ling" Teddy was also offered for sale in the 1930s.

The Chiltern Teddy Bear can be tagged at the side seam; however Chiltern Teddies from the late 1950s can have the label stuck on to the paw pad, together with a cardboard swing tag sewn on to the chest. The tag reads "Chiltern Hygienic Toys Made in England". The swing tag reads "Made in England, Chiltern Toys, Awarded the Certificate of the Institute of Hygiene" on one side and "Trade Mark Chiltern Toys, Made in England", together with the scene of two houses, two trees and a hill on the other.

There are also Teddy Bears bearing tags with both "Chiltern" and "Chad Valley" printed on them indicating these bears were probably made during the takeover period of 1967.

Chiltern Teddy Bears are fully jointed, have glass eyes and are usually kapok filled. Chiltern used a moulded plastic nose on a range of Teddies from the 1950s. Velvet paw pads are also another characteristic of Chiltern Teddies. The firm of Chiltern was taken over by Chad Valley in 1967.

CHINA

Teddy Bears have been reproduced in every conceivable medium (see **Fabric**) (see **Material**) including china. From the early 1900s children's table

ILLUS. 106. The markings on the English baby bowl read "Dolly's School - Grimwades - Made in England".

ILLUS. 105. An early English baby bowl measuring 6 1/2in (16.5cm) across with a transfer print c1920.

ILLUS. 108. An unmarked German made Edwardian piece of bric-a-brac c1910.

BELOW
ILLUS. 109. Part of a breakfast setting depicting transfer prints from Goldilocks and the three bears. The markings on the back of the bowls read "Jas. F. McKenzie Pty Ltd Melbourne, Sydney, Fremantle, Brisbane, England" c1920. Courtesy Ross Schmidt.

BELOW ILLUS. 110. Japanese made plates and mugs depicting white bears c1930s. Courtesy Marjory Fainges.

ILLUS. 107. The markings on the English Teddy baby bowl c1940s. See page 27.(Ilus. 62)

china and miniature toy teasets have been decorated with Teddy Bears. They remain popular subjects today. During the Edwardian period when so much bric-a-brac was produced, items such as match-strikers and bon-bon holders were made in Germany in countless numbers. These cheap little pieces of china often decorated with the then very popular Teddy Bears (beside other cute animals such as pigs) could be found in almost every home. Now very collectable.

CHINESE

The Chinese of Mainland China have been making quality Teddy Bears for approximately forty years. Chinese Teddies can still be found for sale on today's market at very reasonable prices for an attractive serviceable Teddy Bear. The "look" of Chinese-made Teddies has changed very little over the years. The tiny, poor quality, unjointed Teddies (very popular as Christmas tree decorations) have changed somewhat as today's Teddies do have more definition and are a better product than the little cheapie of the 1950s.

However the larger Teddy of the 1940s and 50s is very easy to identify, even though untagged.

The Chinese-made Teddy has large paw pads, usually of a contrasting material to the body fabric, the claws

ONE OF NU-FABRICS 'SPECIALS' FOR 1964!

ILLUS. 112. Chinese Teddy Bears advertised in January 1964 by Melbourne distributors. Courtesy Australasian Sportsgoods and Toy Retailer.

ILLUS. 111. Three Chinese Teddy Bears: the bear on the left is c1950. He has beautiful glass eyes and a moulded rubber nose. The little fellow in the centre is c1960 and he too has glass eyes. The Teddy on the right is available on today's market and features the "safe" plastic clip-in eyes. All three bears are fully jointed, have large paw pads and claws and are very well made.

ILLUS. 113. A cardboard swing tag from a modern Chinese Teddy Bear reads - "Whale - Shanghai Toys Factory No 7 - No SAS 224 - Address 159 Puan Rd Shanghai - Phone 262110 - 261148 - Made in China". The reverse of the tag is gold in colour with circles of red and blue.

40

ILLUS. 114. Two 24in (57cm) Clemens Teddy Bears. Gold mohair, fully jointed, fawn felt paw pads, glass eyes, black embroidered nose, mouth and claws. c1948. Courtesy Marvin Cohen Auctions.

are very large hand-sewn in black with three claws per paw. The eyes on the earlier bear are beautiful quality blown glass. However the Teddies produced today are made with the "safe" lock-in plastic eyes (see **Eyes**). The Chinese Teddy is usually untagged and is marked with the cheaper method of cardboard swing tag tied to the neck ribbon which is very easily lost.

The Teddies of mainland China in today's market wear a cardboard tag that states "Whale Shanghai Toys Factory No 7, Made in China" together with the company's address and phone number in Shanghai. These Teddies have the hand-sewn claws, nose and mouth, are jointed at the shoulders and hips with a stiff neck. They are very firmly filled and the fabric is a dense synthetic plush. A well made toy as were its predecessors. One version of the 1950-60s Teddy has a moulded rubber nose on a longer muzzle.

CHRISTMAS DECORATIONS

Christmas decorations in the shape of Teddies were very popular during the early 1900s. These included glass tree decorations and lights and bon-

bon containers. The early glass lights were made in Europe. However by the 1920s Japan was producing quality glass figured lights. The popularity of these beautiful fragile things diminished in recent years and Teddy Bear Christmas decorations have become as popular as they were in the early 1900s.

CLASSIC TOYS
(see **Humphrey B. Bear**)

CLAWS

Not all Teddy Bears have claws on their paws. Claws cannot be used as an identification aid as replaced claws can be mistaken for originals. Paws that have lost the original claws often appear to have never had claws.

Paws can have three or four claws. One type of Merrythought Teddy Bear has very distinctive claws that start on the back of the paw in the normal way, then the claws are joined together on the pad.

ILLUS. 115. A beautiful Merrythought Teddy Bear, c1950. Note his wrap-around claws on his front paws.

CLEMENS

A company in Kirchardt, West Germany, which has specialised in soft toys and Teddy Bears since 1946. Clemens Teddies are made from the

highest quality mohair and can be fully jointed or soft filled unjointed.

CLOTHES

Teddies are usually attired (if at all) in home-made handknits. However during the early 1900s several American firms commercially produced a wide range of clothes for Teddy Bears. Companies in the United States importing and manufacturing Teddy togs included:

Kahn and Mossbacher
Samstag and Hilder Bros
D. W. Shoyer and Co

The large toy store of F.A. O.Schwarz included clothes for Teddies in their Christmas catalogues through the 1930s and 50s. Costumes available included a fireman's uniform, cowboy and motorist outfit, baseball uniform, clown suit, policeman uniform, ski outfit and overalls.

CLOWNS

Seymour Eaton, the author of "The Roosevelt Bears" (see **Roosevelt Bears**) drew a wonderful clown-dressed bear in his book "Their Travels and Adventures" and perhaps because of this several firms manufactured Clown-Teddies.

These included the American firm of Aetna (see **Aetna**) which sold a fully

ILLUS. 116. A 12in (31cm) tall Chad Valley clown Teddy. Jointed head and arms, his baby shaped body is red mohair and his head is gold mohair. Tagged on the foot "Hygienic Toys, Made in England by Chad Valley Co Ltd." c1920. A rare bear.

ILLUS. 117. Teddy Bear Clothes advertised in The "Ladies Home Journal," December 1907. Courtesy David Worland.

3673—This Teddy-Bear Outfit Consists of a Pajama Suit, Shown on the Left, a Rough-Rider Suit, in the Centre, and a Play Suit, on the Right

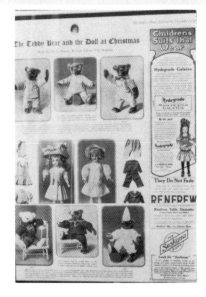

3675—Three Suits for Teddy Bear: on the Left is Shown a Fireman's Suit, in the Centre, a Sailor Suit, and on the Right, a Clown Suit

COLUMBIA TEDDY BEAR MANUFACTURERS

An American company of Teddy bear and soft-toy makers in the early part of the the century. Situated in New York. Well known as the makers of "The Laughing Roosevelt Teddy Bear" in 1907. It is a fully jointed Teddy with an open mouth with white glass teeth. The mouth is opened and closed by means of squeezing the torso. A rare bear.

COMMONWEALTH TOY AND NOVELTY COMPANY

American company, makers of a "Feed Me" Teddy Bear (see **Feed Me Bears**) in 1937. A Panda Bear and rabbit were also made in the "Feed Me" manner.

COMPACT
(see **Novelty**)

COSY TEDDY
A soft filled Teddy by Steiff (see **Steiff**) from 1960s.

COTTON
(see **Fabric**)

ILLUS. 118. Teddy B of "The Roosevelt Bear" by Seymour Eaton in his clown costume in the first of the Teddy B and Teddy G books, "Their Travels and Adventures".

jointed mohair Teddy dressed in a spotted clown outfit very like the Roosevelt Bear Teddy B wears in "Their Travels and Adventures". In the 1920s Sears Roebuck and Company, an American mail-order firm, offered a Clown Bear. The bear, fully jointed with glass eyes is made in red and blue, the left arm blue, the right arm red, the right leg blue, the left leg red. The head is white and the torso is pink and blue seamed down the centre. The bear wore a neck frill. Dean's Childsplay Toys Ltd (see **Dean's Childsplay Toys**) have faithfully reproduced this lovable Teddy as part of the Schoonmaker Signature Series of bears.

COLOURED

The traditional colour for a Teddy is gold. However Teddies have been produced in every colour imaginable. Colour can also be variegated and frosted. Teddies are usually of one colour with perhaps inner ears and paw pads being of a contrasting colour. However, a Teddy Bear thought to be made by Art Novelty Company in 1908 is made in the patriotic colours of red, white and blue.

Teddies made in a combination of black and white are usually called Panda Bears (see **Pandas**).

ILLUS. 119. Cosy Teddy by Steiff, unjointed machine washable. A modern quality toy. Courtesy Steiff.

CROCHET

Teddy Bears have been made in every conceivable medium (see **Fabric** and see **Material**). Patterns for crocheting Teddy Bears have been offered by many women's magazines over the years. The following pattern is taken from an English craft publication c1934.

The Teddy Made in Crochet

Materials:

5 oz Pearl-sheen T 515, 4 ply (sky blue, shade P.11); crochet hook, No 11; stuffing; 2 eyes; a small piece of felt or cloth for soles; 1/2 yard ribbon.

Always turn with 1 ch at ends of rows unless otherwise directed.

The Body

Two Back Pieces (both alike)

Commence at lower edge with 3 chain.

1st row: Miss first ch, 2 dc

2nd row: 2 dc on each dc

3rd row: 2 dc on first dc, 1 dc on each dc to end.

4th row: 1 dc on each dc until 1 remains, 2 dc on last dc.

5th row: 2 dc on first dc, 1 dc on each dc until 1 remains, 2 dc on last dc.

6th row: 1 dc on each dc.

Next 3 rows: As 3rd row.

10th row: As 6th row. Repeat last 6 rows once.

17th row: As 5th row.

Next 17 rows: As 6th row.

35th row: Miss first dc, 1 dc on each dc until 2 remain, 1 dc on last dc.

36th row: As 6th row.

Next 3 rows: Miss first dc, 1 dc on each dc to end.

40th row: As 6th row. Repeat last 6 rows once.

47th row: As 35th row.

48th row: 4 dc, 1 dc on last dc.

49th row: Miss first dc, 4 dc.

50th row: Miss first dc, 1 dc, then 1 dc on last dc, fasten off.

Two Front Pieces (both alike)

Commence with 7 chain.

1st row: Miss first ch, 6 dc.

2nd row: As 5th row of back pieces.

3rd row: 1 dc on each dc.

Next 3 rows: As 4th row of back pieces.

7th row: As 3rd row. Repeat last 6 rows once.

14th row: 2 dc on first dc. 1 dc on each dc to end..

Next 2 rows: As 3rd row.

17th row: 1 dc on each dc until 1 remains, 2 dc on last dc.

Next 17 rows: As 3rd row.

35th row: 1 dc on each dc until 2 remain, 1 dc on last dc.

Next 2 rows: As 3rd row. Repeat last 3 rows once.

41st row: Miss first dc, 1 dc on each dc until 2 remain, 1 dc on last dc.

42nd row: As 35th row.

43rd row: Miss first dc, 1 dc on each dc to end. Repeat 41st, 43rd, 35th, 41st, 35th and 43rd rows respectively.

50th row: Miss first dc, 1 dc, then 1 dc on last dc, fasten off.

Hind Legs (both alike)

Commence with 43 ch.

1st row: Miss first ch, 42 dc.

2nd row: 1 dc on each dc. Repeat last row once.

4th row: Miss first dc, 1 dc on each dc until 2 remain, 1 dc on last dc. Repeat last row 7 times.

12th row: As 2nd row.

13th row: 2 dc on first dc, 1 dc on each dc until 1 remains, 2 dc on last dc. Repeat last 2 rows 4 times (36 dc).

Next 6 rows: As 2nd row.

27th row: As 4th row.

28th row: As 2nd row. Repeat last 2 rows once, then repeat 4th row.

32nd row: 13 dc, 1 ch, turn.

33rd row: As 4th row.

34th row: 9 dc, 1 dc on last dc, fasten off. Miss 4 dc along centre of 32nd row, then 13 dc on 13 dc.

33rd row: As 4th row.

34th row: Miss first dc, 10 dc, fasten off.

Forelegs (both alike)

*Commence at top with 9 chain.

1st row: Miss first ch, 8 dc.

2nd row: 2 dc on first dc, 1 dc on each dc until 1 remains, 2 dc on last dc* Break off wool and fasten off. Leave this piece and repeat from * to *.

3rd row: 9 dc, 2 dc on last dc, 4 ch, take up the piece that was left and work 2 dc on first dc, 9 dc.

4th row: 2 dc on first dc, 1 dc on each stitch until 1 remains, 2 dc on last dc.

5th row: As 4th row.

6th row: 1 dc on each dc. Repeat last 2 rows once (32 dc).

Next 2 rows: As 6th row.

11th row: Miss first dc, 1 dc on each dc until 2 remain, 1 dc on last dc.

Next 3 rows: As 6th row. Repeat last 4 rows 3 times, then repeat 11th row.

28th row: 9 dc, turn.

29th row: 3 ss, 6 dc.

30th row: 3 dc, fasten off. Miss 2 dc along centre of 28th row, then work 11 dc on 11 dc.

29th row: Miss first dc, 1 dc on each dc.

30th row: As 6th row. Repeat last 2 rows twice. Repeat 11th row 3 times, fasten off.

Two Side-pieces for Head (both alike)

Commence with 19 chain.

1st row: Miss first ch, 18 dc.

2nd row: 1 dc on each dc until 1 remains, 2 dc on last dc.

3rd row: 2 dc on first dc, 1 dc on each dc.

4th row: As 2nd row.

5th row: 2 dc on first dc, 1 dc on each dc until 1 remains, 2 dc on last dc. Repeat 2nd, 3rd and 2nd rows respectively. Repeat last 4 rows once then repeat 3rd row.

14th row: Miss first dc, 1 dc on each dc until 1 remains, 2 dc on last dc (32 dc).

15th row: 1 dc on each dc.

16th row: Miss first dc, 1 dc on each dc until 2 remain, turn.

17th row: 2ss, 1 dc on each dc.

18th row: Miss first dc, 1 dc on each dc until 2 remain, 1 dc on last dc, turn. Repeat 17th, 16th, 18th and 16th rows respectively.

23rd row: 2 ss, 1 dc on each dc until 2 remain, 1 dc on last dc.

24th row: As 18th row.

25th row: As 23rd row, fasten off.

Centre Head

Commence at lower edge with 7 chain.

1st row: Miss first ch, 6 dc.

2nd row: 1 dc on each dc.

3rd row: 2 dc on first dc, 1 dc on each dc until 1 remains, 2 dc on last dc.

Next 2 rows: As 2nd row. Repeat last 3 rows 6 times (20 dc).

24th row: As 2nd row.

25th row: Miss first dc, 1 dc on each dc until 2 remain, 1 dc on last dc.

Next 2 rows: As 2nd row. Repeat last 3 rows 5 times.

43rd row: As 25th row, fasten off.

The Ears (both alike)

Commence with 13 chain.

1st row: Miss first ch, 12 dc.

Next 3 rows: 12 dc

Next 3 rows: Miss first dc, 1 dc on each dc until 2 remain, 1 dc on last dc.

8th row: 6 dc.

Next 3 rows: 2 dc on first dc, 1 dc on each dc, 2 dc on last.

Next 3 rows: 12 dc, fasten off.

To Make Up

Pin out each piece, and press. Cut 10 cardboard buttons 1 1/2 inches across. Sew up leg seams. Cut 2 pieces of cardboard for soles 3 inches long and 2 inches wide, and round corners off, cover with felt and sew to base of legs. Stuff legs firmly, then insert at top of each a cardboard button, pierced in centre with a two-pronged paper fastener an inch long. Place in position and sew with head of fastener next to inside. Sew up arm seams, cut 2 paws in felt and sew in position, then stuff firmly and sew 2 cardboard buttons at top as described for legs. Sew up body seams. Place legs in position on body then insert a cardboard button inside body where legs are to be attached, pass prongs extending from top of legs through centre of button inside, then press prongs open. Fix arms in the same way as legs, then stuff body firmly and place a cardboard button at neck. Sew centre piece to sides of head, leaving a space at top open for stuffing. Sew up neck and place a button inside head. Pass the prongs of the neck button through head button, press prongs open, then stuff head firmly and sew up opening. Sew on ears. Mark nose, mouth and divisions for paws with black wool. Fix eyes into position.

D

DAKIN R. AND COMPANY
Founded in 1955 by R. Y. Dakin, firstly as importers and distributors of toys and sporting goods, now produces soft toys in USA, Japan, Hong Kong and Mexico. The Dakin Company makes over fifty varieties of Teddies in all sizes.

R. Dakin and Company made the Misha Olympic Teddy. (see **Misha**) Popular Teddies made by R. Dakin and Company include:

Bentley Bear
Gramps
Pudgsy Polar Bear
Pumpkin Bear
Super Huggy
Twinkle Toes

R. Dakin and Company. took over House of Nisbet doll and Teddy Bear making company in 1989 (see **House of Nisbet**).

ILLUS. 121. Dakin Toys advertisement c1983. Courtesy Australasian Sportsgoods and Toy Retailer.

ILLUS. 120. "Gramps" by Dakin. 19in (48cm) tall, fully jointed, "Gramps" wears a red check scarf and spectacles. A leather tag around his neck reads "Elegante by Dakin". A cloth tag sewn into his left leg seam reads "© 1983 Dana McCallum. R. Dakin and Co, San Francisco, CA PA Reg 118/. All new materials Contents synthetic/natural fibres. Made in USA". "Gramps" is typical of the high quality character bears made by Dakin.

DEAN'S CHILDSPLAY TOYS
This great English firm of toymakers was established in 1903, as Dean's Rag Book Company Ltd.

The company's famous trademark of two dogs fighting over a cloth book was registered in 1910.

Lithographed cut- and- sew toys were a big part of the company's early range of products. In the 1920s pulla-long animals were also produced as well as soft toy animals, Golliwoggs and Teddy Bears.

Dean's Childsplay Toys of England manufactured the first Mickey Mouse for Walt Disney. The company has had many addresses since 1903. It was founded by Samuel Dean, in Fleet

ILLUS. 123. Top Dean's tag c1938. Centre and lower Dean's tag c1970.

3 DEAN'S CHILDSPLAY TOYS LIMITED

RIGHT ILLUS. 122. The Dean's Childsplay Toys Ltd stand at the Sydney Toy Fair in 1970. Courtesy Australasian Sportsgoods and Toy Retailer.

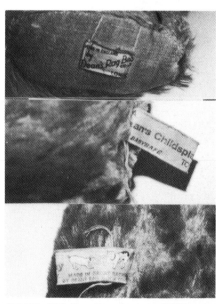

ILLUS. 124. A wonderful Dean's cloth dog c1915 16in (41cm) tall by 12in(31cm) long. The features are moulded and painted. Glass eyes, unjointed, cork filled. He is marked around his neck.

ILLUS.125."Dean's Trutolife Animals, Made in England. Patent No 25451 USA 15th April 1915". "Trade Mark Regd All Countries, Hygienic Stuffing Guaranteed" is printed on the neck of the Dean's Cloth Bulldog.

Street, London. Then moved to the Elephant and Castle area, where the trademark of two fighting dogs was used to show the factory's whereabouts.
In 1956 the company left London for Sussex and in 1974 moved to additional premises in Pontypool in South Wales. At this time Dean's Childsplay Toys company merged with

Dean's Rag Book Co.
Dean's also produced "Collector Bears" one of which is the "Schoonmaker Bears" (see **Clowns**) replicas of Patricia Schoonmaker's own original Teddy Bears.
In 1982 the Sussex factory closed, and in 1988 the company was taken over and the trading name is no longer in use.
The beautiful early bears of the English firm are very collectable. They carry a label sewn to the foot, with the words, "Made in England by Dean's Rag Book Co Ltd, London". They are fully jointed, made from quality mohair, kapok stuffed and have glass eyes.

DELICATESSEN
(see **Aloysius**)
(see **Bull, Peter**)

DEMUSA
An East Germany Government company, established in the early 1950s, distributor of musical instruments, games, dolls and plush toys including Teddy Bears. Quality fully jointed Teddy Bears made in Thuringia.

ILLUS. 126. The Demusa representative at the 1966 Sydney Toy Fair, with part of the Demusa range . Courtesy Australasian Sportsgoods and Toy Retailer.

ILLUS. 127 Advertisement for East German firm of Demusa c1965. Courtesy Australasian Sportsgoods and Toy Retailer.

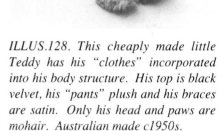

ILLUS.128. This cheaply made little Teddy has his "clothes" incorporated into his body structure. His top is black velvet, his "pants" plush and his braces are satin. Only his head and paws are mohair. Australian made c1950s.

DICKY

A smiling Teddy Bear made by Steiff (see **Steiff**) in 1930 and re-issued in the early 1980s as a limited edition collector's Teddy. Dicky is fully jointed, has a mohair coat with a shaved muzzle and velvet pads with paws printed on them. A popular different looking Teddy.

DOLL TEDDY
(see **Teddy Dolls**)

DRALON

A synthetic plush used in Teddy Bear making since the 1960s.

DRESSED BEARS

Over the years many companies have manufactured "Dressed" Teddy Bears, Teddy Bears that have clothing incorporated into the body structure (the clothing is not removable). One of the most collectable of these Teddies must be the "Yes-No Bellhop Bear" by Schuco (see **Schuco**). His red jacket and black pants are part of the body structure. Other Teddy Bears made in this manner include Merrythought's "Beefeater" (see **Beefeater**).

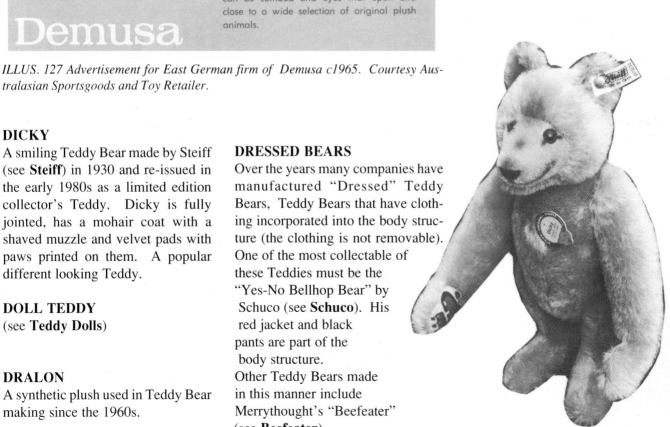

ILLUS. 129. The reissued "Dicky" by Steiff.

47

10M20

BEAR AND RABBIT in fancy waistcoats and striped pants—great fun for playpen or pram. Soft rayon plush, made in England. Bear in pastel colours, rabbit in white only. Both 12½″ tall. *Packed: 12 ozs.* . . . . . . **18′11**

ILLUS. 131. A dressed bear and bunny c1950. Courtesy David Jones.

The Australian Home Beautiful,
October, 1955

PRIVILEGE TOY PATTERN OFFER
A postal note for 2/6 and the coupon overleaf brings you full-scale pattern and complete instructions for making 19in. high Teddy Bear (with money-box drum) from colorful felt.

ILLUS. 130. A dressed Teddy to make. An offer from the "Australian Home Beautiful", October 1955. Courtesy June Hayes.

Rupert Bear (see **Rupert Bear**) made by many companies and "Smokey Bear" (see **Smokey Bear**)

Perhaps many companies made "dressed" bears during times of economic pressure as the "pants" or "jackets" of the Teddy Bear would probably cost less than the expensive mohair resulting in a more cost effective Teddy.

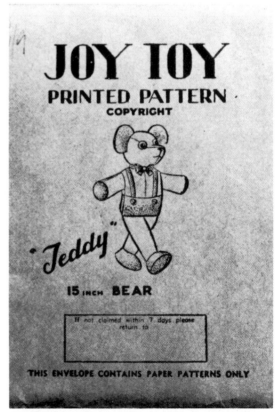

ILLUS. 132. An Australian war time pattern for a dressed bear put out by the Joy Toys company c1942.

EARS

Teddy Bears usually have them. "Cheeky" by Merrythought has bells in the ears (see **Cheeky**).

Steiff bears are all tagged in the ear with a button "Knopf Im Ohr" (see **Steiff**)

Merrythought and Chad Valley have also marked their Teddy Bears with buttons in the ear at some time. (see **Buttons**)

Ears can be sewn on to the head or inserted into a slit in the head. Ears cannot be used as a method of identifying manufacturer's name.

ILLUS. 133. A 26in (68cm) Teddy Bear. Fully jointed with a shaved muzzle, large brown glass eyes, felt paw pads. Tagged to the foot with a label reading Peacocks British Toys London 1927 - 1930. Courtesy Christies Auctions, South Kensington.

EDEN TOYS

An American company that manufactures in Korea and best known for their production of Paddington Bear. (see **Paddington**)

ELECTRO

"Electro" Teddy Bear, c1914, sold in USA for $2.25. "Electro" had battery-driven glass bulb eyes that shone. By pressing a button in the torso the electric bulb eyes would flash and were guaranteed "good for 6,000 flashes".

ELEPHANT BUTTON

This term refers to a type of button found in the ear of some Steiff Teddy Bears. The buttons are metal, and imprinted with an elephant with a raised trunk.

This button is found on some Steiff Teddies made in 1904-1905.

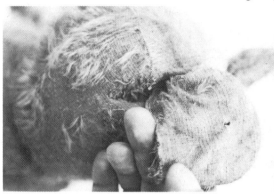

ILLUS. 134. An early Teddy c1930s - note the ears are sliced into the head. This method is popular with Japanese Teddy makers.

ELVIS PRESLEY TEDDY BEAR

Made by Coronet Toy Manufacturers of Seattle, Washington, USA, in the early 1970s. A 10in (25cm) unjointed soft filled Teddy of black and white synthetic plush. This Teddy wears a large badge picturing Elvis, around the edge of the badge "Elvis Summer Festival Sahara, Tahoe, RCA Records". A rare Teddy given by Elvis to a small select group of people, including employees.

ENGLISH TEDDY BEARS

One of the first English firms to produce mohair jointed Teddy Bears was the firm of J. K. Farnell (see **Farnell, Alpha**). Dean's Childsplay Toys also manufactured Teddies before 1920 (see **Dean's Childs play Toys**). Within a few years many firms were producing beautiful

ILLUS. 135. Steiff Elephant-button bear, c1904. 16in (41cm) tall in near mint condition. This rare bear is fully jointed with rods, is complete with his button and has his original wax nose. Courtesy David Worland.

quality Teddy Bears; in fact the early J. K. Farnell Teddies were exported to Germany in competition with German products.

English-made Teddy Bears were made for the local market and for export to many countries, especially Commonwealth countries. Usually of high quality and imaginative design, English Teddies do have characteristics that make them uniquely English.

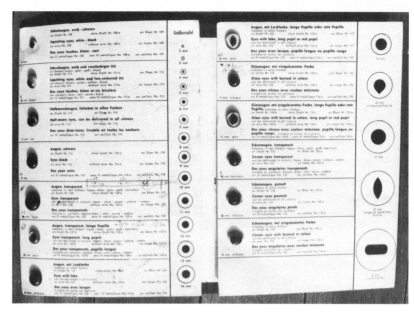

ILLUS. 137. A German catalogue of glass Teddy Bear and soft toy's eyes, c1930s. Thirteen glass eye samples are in the catalogue. They include "squinting eyes, black eyes, transparent eyes, eyes with long pupils, eyes with lakes, corner eyes." The catalogue states the eyes are available in several colours and sizes, with or without wires or on loops. The catalogue has no maker's name on it and it is printed in German, English and French. It was sent to an import company in Melbourne.

ILLUS. 136. An English Teddy Bear, maker unknown. The bear is tagged Made In England. Note the broad head and the oil cloth (rexine) paw pads c1940s.

The early English-made Teddies were excelsior filled but kapok was in use by 1930. The paws and heads of English bears can be filled with excelsior and the limbs and torso kapok filled.

The paw pads on English Teddies are usually made from velvet or different types of oil cloth including "rexine"; however the very early examples of English Teddies had felt paw pads.

English Teddies usually have plumper torsos, shorter arms and smaller, rounder feet than German or American-made Teddies of the same era. Broad heads, large ears and large

10X11: Teddy Bear of finest English fur fabric. Movable head, limbs, squeaks. 12" tall Pkd.: 12 ozs., 31 –

1952

10X11

UA40S 1948

UA40S—English Fur Fabric Teddy Bears, with glass eyes. Sizes and prices: 15", 28/6; 17", 35/-; 21", 47/6.

1949

10G8

10G8 : 12 inch high English teddy in gold fur fabric. Glass eyes, leather pad, squeak. 20 Postage : N.S.W. 1/-, Interstate 1/6, Far States 2

6'6

1930

TEDDY BEAR - 6/6
The "Chiltern" Teddy Bear, of high grade English make. Growlers and Squeakers.
Sizes: 10 12 13½ 15
Prices: 6/6 8/6 10/6 11/9
16 19 20 22 24
13/6 18/6 22/6 25/- 27/6

UA206Y

1949

UA206Y—English Teddy Bears, Golden Brown with Squeaker; 16in. high. Price, each. 35/9

UA227D

UA227D — English long h Teddy Bear, Golden Bro Sizes: 15in., 34/11; 17in., 45 21in., 54/6.

1947

ILLUS. 136a. English Teddy Bears advertised in various Christmas catalogues.

ILLUS.140. Two Emil Teddies c1950s. Jointed at the shoulders and hips, vinyl paw pads, glass eyes, black nose and mouth. Tagged in the back centre seam.

ILLUS. 138. Very sweet English mohair Teddy Bear, maker unknown c1940s

eyes are also a feature of English Teddies.

Many Teddy Bear makers are still manufacturing high quality products today in England. Well known English Teddy Bear manufacturers include:

Canterbury Bears (see **Canterbury Bears**)

Chad Valley (see **Chad Valley**)
Chiltern (see **Chiltern**)
Dean's (see **Dean's Childsplay Toys**)
J. K. Farnell (see **Farnell, Alpha**)
House of Nisbet (see **House of Nisbet**)
Merrythought (see **Merrythought**)
Pedigree (see **Pedigree**)

EMIL

An Australian company, manufacturers of soft toys including Teddy Bears and panda bears from the 1930s until the 1970s. The early Teddies were of a quality mohair, fully jointed with glass eyes and velvet paw pads. The later Teddies have stiff necks. Emil Teddies carry a tag in either a side or back seam, stating "Emil Toys Made in Australia". The tag is in white satin and the writing is printed in blue, a Teddy is sitting on the letter "E" of the Emil.

ILLUS. 141. The Emil Toys printed cloth tag.

ESKIMO DOLLS
(see **Teddy Dolls**)

Plush Eskimos.
Assorted Colours.

ILLUS.139. A group of English Teddy Bears from the 1940-50s. Note the large ears and broad heads.

ILLUS. 142. Taken from a Faudels Ltd, London Christmas catalogue c1911.

ILLUS. 143. A rare 25in (40cm) electric eye Teddy Bear. The battery is sewn into the back of the head. The eyes are operated by pressing an area under the left ear. This wonderful bear is fully jointed, excelsior filled and made from quality mohair. The paw-pads are felt and the nose, mouth and claws are fawn coloured. Maker uknown, c1920s. The inset shows the eyes lit up.

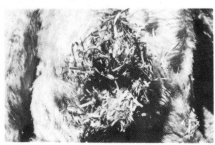

ILLUS.144. Excelsior wood shavings, used in filling some Teddy Bears and other soft toys until the use of new "hygienic filling".

EXCELSIOR

First used as a trade name by an English company for shaved wood used as a filling. Now in common usage to describe any type of shaved wood filling.

Bears said to be "straw filled" are in fact filled with shaved wood-excelsior. The earliest examples of excelsior were finer than they are today.

The German toy manufacturers favoured the excelsior filling. However most Teddy Bears are now filled with "Hygienic Filling" of new material. English and Australian-made Teddy Bears were usually flock or kapok filled with only the nose and paws stuffed with the more durable excelsior.

EYES

Teddy Bears' eyes, are usually brown in colour. The first eyes used were the black shoe-button type. By 1906 glass eyes were in use. They were made of blown glass on wire shanks. Some English companies used glass eyes with a metal loop moulded into the glass, enabling the eye to be sewn on to the head (see **Farnell Alpha**). This type of eye was known as a "safety first eye".

The glass eyes used in English-made Teddy Bears were usually plain with the back of the eye painted brown. Over the years the colour can be lost causing the eye to be plain glass.

Some Teddies do have blue eyes but predominantly Teddy Bears have brown eyes. One Australian-made Teddy (see **Lindee**) had green eyes. However Australian-made Teddy Bears usually had beautiful brown blown glass eyes on wire shanks made in China. These eyes can still be bought today .

In 1926 Schuco advertised a line of soft toy animals, including Teddy Bears with "Sparkling Eyes".

Eyes have also been made from tin and celluloid. A Teddy sold under the name of "Electro" (see **Electro**) had flashing electric eyes. Ideal also manufactured an electric-eye Bear in 1919. Today the safer lock-in plastic eyes are mainly used.

In an article on soft toys in an issue of "Games and Toys, UK" in 1960, K.

B. Williams the Chairman and Managing Director of Wendy Boston Playsafe Toys Ltd, states "that no reputable manufacturers used glass eyes in toys today". In the next issue the Editor commented that "reputable manufacturers embodied glass eyes in their production and that with modern methods of fixing there is no doubt that they are just as safe as plastic eyes. Any part of a toy is unsafe if improperly applied". Courtesy Australasian Sportsgoods and Toy Retailer.

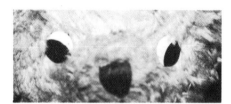

ILLUS. 145. Painted tin eyes found on some cotton plush Polish-made Teddies of the 1960s.

ILLUS. 146. Celluloid eyes in an unmarked German bear.

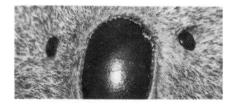

ILLUS. 147. Shoe-button eyes in an early Koala Bear c1930s.

ILLUS. 148. The glass eyes on the Dean's Teddy Bear are backed with a circle of black felt c1950s.

F

FABRIC

Teddy Bears have been made in almost every imaginable fabric. The most popular and the traditional fabric for Teddy is gold mohair plush. Many types of synthetic plush are now used. Other fabrics used in commercial manufacture over the years include:

ILLUS. 149. 16in (41cm) Alpha Farnell Teddy Bear. Fully jointed, long gold mohair fabric, rexine paw pads, kapok filling, plastic clip-in eyes . Tagged to the torso centre seam, c1960s. These later Alpha Farnell Teddies have black embroidered noses and plastic eyes, the tag can be in the side or the centre torso seam.

Inset. The tag of the 1960s Alpha Farnell Teddy. Made of white rayon with the information printed in red and blue. The tag reads "A Farnell Alpha Hygienic Toy - Made in England."

ILLUS. 150. This beautiful 14in (36cm) Kestner 143 bisque head doll wears a "Teddy Bear Coat and Hat" made from gold mohair plush fabric. She holds a 3 1/2in (9cm) Steiff Teddy c1950s. Courtesy L. Albright.

Alpaca
Angora mohair
Art silk plush
Cloth, cut-and-sew type Teddy
Cotton Plush
Felt
Fur
Homemade Teddies have been knitted, crocheted and made from old clothes, bedding, quilts and anything else handy at the time.
Kangaroo Skin
Sail cloth
Sheepskin
Towelling
Wool Worsted

FARNELL, J.K.

Started to produce toys in 1897 in

ILLUS. 151. A 1940s Alpha Farnell Teddy. Fully jointed, kapok filled, gold mohair coat.

London, England. Manufactured top quality Teddy Bears as early as 1904 to be exported to Germany.

Produced Teddy Bears made from mohair, art silk plush, alpaca and nylon plush.

Originator of the "safety first eye". a glass eye made without a metal shank. (see **Eyes**)

The Alpha Farnell bears included bears made with rattles, musical chimes and growlers, and the company manufactured Teddy Bears exclusively for Harrods of London.

The original "Winnie the Pooh" Teddy Bear (see **Winnie the Pooh**) was bought from Harrods and is thought to have been an Alpha Farnell Teddy Bear.

ILLUS. 152. A "Farnell-Alpha Toy - Made in England" tag c 1920s.

The earlier Alpha Farnell Teddy Bear had traditional black stitched nose

ILLUS. 154.An early 17 1/2in (45cm) Alpha Farnell Teddy Bear thought to be the type sold to Harrods Department Store in London in the early 1900s. Courtesy Mason Gray Strange Auctioneers, Sydney.

54

and claws. However some early types of Farnell Teddy Bears have the nose, mouth and claws stitched from a light tan coloured cotton thread.

Cloth tagged to the foot "Farnell Alpha Toys - Made in England".

Alpha Farnell also produced soft toy animals and cloth dolls. The company was sold in 1968.

ILLUS. 153. A 1950s Alpha Farnell Teddy, the limbs are shorter and fatter, the head broader.

FATHER BEAR

Head of the house in the Three Bears' household (see **The Three Bears**.)

FEED ME BEARS

Perhaps this term can be applied to any Teddy Bear with a mechanically operated open and closing mouth, whether it has a receptacle for holding "food" in the torso or not.

The Commonwealth Toy and Novelty Company of the USA produced a "Feed Me" Teddy in 1937 for The National Biscuit Company. This Teddy had a metal ring affixed to the top of his head. When the ring was pulled the Teddy's mouth would open and biscuits etc could be "eaten". A

metal compartment in the torso held the "food". The compartment could be reached through a zippered opening in the back.

Many firms manufactured Teddy Bears with apparatus in the head which enables the Teddy's mouth to open and close, simulating talking or eating. These bears do not have containers in the torso.

FILLING

As Teddies are made in many fabrics and materials, so they are filled with many different fillings.

The early German and American made Teddy Bears were stuffed with excelsior (see **Excelsior**). English Teddy Bear makers had a preference for using kapok or cotton flock in their early bears. Australian manufacturers preferred kapok and then, in the 1940s and 50s, rubber.

Other fillings used included cork, sawdust and wool. The law now demands that children's toys be filled with new hygienic filling, as recycled shredded fabrics from used mat-

ILLUS.155.A "Feed-me" type Teddy with a very long muzzle. The top and bottom of the mouth moves open and closed when a mechanism in the torso is pressed. 14in(36cm) tall, glass eyes, oil cloth paw pads, jointed limbs. c1950s.

ILLUS. 156. Two "Feed-me" type Teddies, by the same maker. Fully jointed 16in (41cm) tall, plump body and limbs and a broad head indicate English maker c1950. The paw pads are oil cloth, the eyes glass. These Teddies have an open mouth that can be made to open wide and close by means of two little glass knobs in the back of the head.

ILLUS. 157.   Courtesy "Games and Toys" English trade magazine c1950.

LEFT
ILLUS. 158. Most unhygienic filling from an unmarked English Teddy c1920s. This filling includes string, carpet fibres, animal hair, wood chip, cotton waste and many pieces of unidentified material.

tresses, carpets and clothing have been found to be used as filling for children's toys in years gone by.

FLOCK
Cotton or wool flock can be used to fill soft toys including Teddy Bears. Flock is the refuse, the fibre left after sorting. However cotton flock can refer to waste cotton fabric that is shredded and used as filling.

FRED AND FEE FEE BEARS
Dressed Teddies made by the soft toy making firm of L.J. Sterne. (see **Humphrey B. Bear**.)

FRENCH TEDDY BEARS
During the late 1890s and early 1900s the French firms of Roullet et De-camps (see **Roullet et Decamps**)

ILLUS. 160. A French mechanical bear by Roullet et Decamps 7in (18cm) tall c 1878. Courtesy Christie's Auctions, South Kensington.

coloured paw pads and inner ears.
An innovative French Teddy Bear maker was the company Alfa (Articles de Luxe et de Fabrication Artisanole). In 1937 they released a Teddy with jointed arms and head but with stiff legs.

In 1954 foam rubber was in use as filling in some French manufactured Teddies including bears made by the Boulgon Company. These bears were made jointed and unjointed.

Sheepskin was a popular material used in Teddy Bear making in France during and after World War II when manufactured materials were unavailable.

Most vintage French Teddy Bears are unmarked.

FUR

Teddy Bears are usually made from make believe fur fabric (see **Fabric**) However some Teddy Bears made from real fur have been manufactured. These include Teddies made from mink.

The French firm of Roullet et Decamps (see **Roullet et Decamps**) used rabbit fur on some of their products.

FURSKIN BEARS

Character Teddy Bears created by Xavier Roberts of Cabbage Patch fame of the USA. These delightful

ILLUS. 161. Fred and Fee Fee Bears, made by L. J. Sterne of Melbourne c1965. Unjointed, synthetic plush, plastic eyes and moulded plastic nose. These charming Teddies were only marked on their removable clothes, so if they are lost the bears became "maker unknown". Courtesy L.J. Sterne.

made mechanical wind-up bears. However production of Teddy Bears in France did not commence until after World War I. Up until that time Teddy Bears were imported, mainly from Germany.

It is believed that the first company to make Teddies in France was the Thiennot company, who commenced business in 1919, then producing Teddy Bears. This company made prize-winning Teddy Bears for some years.

Teddy Bears manufactured in France during the 1920s tend to have a larger torso than German bears and the ears are usually larger in proportion to the head and sit rather high. French Teddy makers favour contrasting

RIGHT
ILLUS. 162. Purchased in France in 1985. 28in (71cm) tall, fully jointed, open mouth laughing Teddy. Cream cloth paw pads and inner mouth, gold plush, glass eyes.

contemporary Teddies can be easily identified by their large moulded vinyl boots. Can be made in China (see ILLUS. 29. for photograph of Dudley Furskin).

RIGHT
ILLUS. 163. A key wind mechanical dancing bear by the French firm of Roullet et Decamps. 12in (31cm) tall, made from metal covered in rabbit fur, the paws are papier - mache, the eyes are blue glass. The moulded nose is missing. The key is attached to the back of the bear and is marked R.D. c1890.

BELOW LEFT
ILLUS. 164. 24in (61cm) tall fully jointed Teddy with large celluloid eyes. This Teddy is made with the long body and limbs found in early French made Teddy Bears.
BELOW RIGHT
ILLUS. 165. A fully jointed sheepskin Teddy Bear, shoe-button eyes, suede leather nose and paw pads. Thought to be French, maker unknown c1930s.

58

GABRIELLE
(see **Paddington**)

GARRUMP
A character in a children's story by Australian author Jim Picton-Warlow, illustrated by Margaret Benoit. The hero is the oh so elegant, charming bear Garrump.

GBN
(see **Bing, Gebrüder**)

GERMAN TEDDY BEARS
The number of known German Teddy Bear makers is very large. However, we will probably never know the full number of large and small firms involved in the Teddy Bear making industry in Germany. A peculiarity of the German soft-toy making industry is the large number of "home-workers" or "out-workers" that are used (people that work in their own homes making products for a company that are then sold under the company's name). With most of the workers working in their own homes there was no need for a factory building and so many firms could operate as toy makers without the large financial backing needed to buy and maintain factory buildings and machinery.

This still applies today and Bonnie H. Moore reported in "Teddy Bear and Friends", August 1986 that the German firm of Grisly (see **Grisly**) employed 40 to 50 people, all "out-workers". The company is run from the small family home. The Hermann company also operates in this manner today, employing many "out-workers". Perhaps this is one of the reasons for the proliferation of German soft-toy makers. Whatever the reason Germany had some of the finest soft-toy makers in the world.

We who are interested in Teddy Bears are very familiar with the well-known names of the early German Teddy makers. These include:
Bing (see Bing, **Gebrüder**)
Hermann (see **Hermann Gebr KG**)
Schuco (see **Schuco**)
Steiff (see **Steiff**)
However for every well-known German Teddy maker there are so many that are either not well known or not known at all.

Research by Jürgen and Marianne Cieslik in recent years on the great doll makers of Germany has also brought to light many firms that made or distributed Teddy Bears as well as dolls.

Peter C. Kalinke in his report in "Teddy Bear and Friends" in October 1987 states that in the early 1900s

ILLUS 166. A group of German made Teddies and a friend. Courtesy Phillips Fine Art Auctioneers, U.K.

many German plush toy makers were producing up to 100 bears a day using local village workers in the "out-worker" system. At that time, according to Mr Kalinke, there were 19 better-known plush toy makers in the Neustadt-Sonneberg area producing up to 1900 Teddy Bears a day. By 1930 more than 40 plush toymakers made Teddy Bears in that area. Many, many thousands of Teddy Bears were made in Germany to be exported all over the world. Not all of them were made from quality products and not many of them were marked with a maker's name (see **Un-marked**).

Listed are names of German firms that advertised Teddy Bears for sale.

Büchner, Oskar - Ebersdorf
1925 referred to as a maker of Dolls, Dummies and cloth toys.
The Büchner trademark was a Teddy Bear holding the letters O B inside a triangle.

Buschow, Wilhelm - Dresden
1926 advertised numerous types of doll and Teddy Bears.

Cresco-Spielwarenfabrik GmbH - Schweinfurt
1920 advertised dancing dolls and Teddy Bears.

Dehler, E - Coburg
1906 advertised plush animals.
1911 used a sample card showing dolls and Teddy Bears.

Deuerlein Nachf, Josef
1910 produced plush animals.
1907 used a trademark of a Teddy Bear in a circle holding a banner "Hercules".
1907 used a trademark of a Teddy Bear stepping out while pulling an elephant on wheels that has a monkey on its back. Teddy holds a banner **"Kolundro".**

Dressel and Pietschmann - Coburg
1923 used a trademark of a doll, a Santa Claus carrying a Christmas tree and a sitting and standing Teddy Bear.

Fleischmann and Bloedel - Sonneberg, Paris and London
1914 used a trademark of a doll and a Teddy Bear dancing.

Forster, Albert - Coburg
1929 the trademark of this company incorporated the "AF" together with a striding Teddy.

Forster, Gustav - Coburg
1925 advertisement for this firm included dolls, soft toys, a Teddy Bear on wheels and a Teddy Bear.

Hahn & Company - Nuremberg

1921 registered trademark "Hanco" for "plush bears, cloth animals, knock-about dolls".
The trademark was a Teddy Bear breaking through a globe of the world waving a banner "Hanco-Nürnberg" "Schutz-Marke" under the globe.

Harmus, Carl Jr. - Sonneberg
1909 registered trademark is a Teddy Bear holding a doll inside a triangle.
1912 advertised a character doll and a dressed Teddy Bear.

Hoffmeister, Carl - Sonneberg
1923 reported to have ceased manufacturing leather and artificial leather dolls and producing "only softly stuffed animals and Teddies".

Horn, Carl - Nachf
1928 advertised miniature dolls, dolls for doll houses. The advertisement shows a Teddy Bear.

Jügelt, Walter - Coburg
1923 used a trademark showing a doll with a bear on all fours.

Kohler and Rosenwald - Nuremberg
1925 used as a trademark the figure of a bear standing on one foot holding a banner together with "Kolundro".

Krauth, Werner - Leipzig
1920 used a trademark of dolls and a bear holding hands and dancing

ILLUS. 167. Teddies by Steiff and Schuco and unknown German makers. Courtesy Phillips Fine Art Auctioneers, U.K. .

ILLUS.168. An early 8in (20cm) Teddy Bear glove puppet. Shoe-button eyes, maker unknown. The Teddy is an early Steiff. Courtesy Christie's Auctions South Kensington.

around a globe of the world.

Leven and Sprenger - Sonneberg
1930 a catalogue page of the company shows a number of soft toys including a dog, donkey, Teddy-Doll, elephant and a Teddy Bear as well as bisque-head dolls.

Luthard, Louis Philipp - Coburg
1921 advertised "Cloth animals, bears, eskimos" etc. Their trademark was a Teddy and a doll standing on a horizontal "L" with a "P".

Müller, Andreas - Sonneberg
1922 used a trademark of a doll and a Teddy and a jester together with the words "Spielmüller Coburg"

Rogner, Hermann Nachf - Nuremberg
1926 in an advertisement mentioned Teddy Bears.

Scheyer and Company - Nuremberg
1920 registered trademark "FLORESTA" for "Dolls and toys." 1925 advertised "Toys of felt and plush, dolls, babies. Trademark "FLORESTA" Registered trademark "Mafuka" for plush toys, dolls and animals."

Schmey, Gustav - Sonneberg and Coburg
1911 a trademark showing several different types of bisque-head dolls, plush animals including a cat, dog, sheep, monkey and donkey, wheeled toy horses and a Teddy standing on all fours.

Schmidt, Eduard - Coburg

1925 advertised "Sico, Sicora Wonder dolls and Teddies. Sicora dolls and Sicora Teddies walk with the registered 'Sicora' walking shoe even on the the slickest linoleum floor. 'Sicora' Wonder doll and 'Sicora' Wonder Teddies attract attention, especially with the 'Sicora' Walking Stick".
Their trademark was a wonderful Teddy stepping out.

Schunk, Wilhelm - Coburg
1926 advertised "Mechanical walking device for Teddy Bears, dolls and clowns".

Steiner, Hermann - Coburg
1929 advertised on a trade card "Rolf the darlings Teddy Bear".

Strunz, Wilhelm - Nuremberg
1911 used a trademark of a standing bear.

Waldes & Company - Dresden
1927 advertised "Connection for doll joints, toys, especially for stuffed toys like Teddy Bears and similar".

Wohlmann, Otto - Nuremberg
1913 used a trademark of a standing bear with the initials "OWN - for Toys of cloth, felt and plush".

So many other German toy making firms also mention "soft toys", "fur animals", "animal figures". These could refer to Teddy Bears. I have only noted the firms that mentioned Teddy Bears or include Teddy Bears in trade cards, trademarks or advertising that can be found in J. & M. Cieslik's "German Doll Encyclopedia 1800-1939".

GLOVE PUPPETS

Operating glove puppets has been a popular form of entertainment for centuries. Glove puppets have been made depicting all types of human and animal characters.
Since the early part of this century the Teddy Bear has been a popular subject for glove puppets.
The Teddy Bear glove puppet has a partially hollow head on an empty body. Arms are attached to the body

and these too are empty. Teddy Bear glove puppets do not usually have legs.

10E27: HAND PUPPETS in soft fur fabric. Dogs, tigers, monkeys and bears with full moulded heads. For 4 to 12 years. 18 ozs. **10/6**

ILLUS.169. Advertisement Christmas 1959. Courtesy David Jones, Sydney.

The hand is placed inside the body with the fingers in the head and the arms, enabling the Teddy Bear glove puppet to be manipulated into life-like antics.
Companies that manufactured Teddy Bear glove puppets include Steiff and Chiltern. Merrythought manufactured several different types of glove puppets, one a panda, but no Teddy Bear glove puppets appear in their catalogues.
In 1950 Chad Valley of England

ILLUS. 170. This 19in (48cm) Berlex Teddy is holding a glove puppet. The puppet is unmarked and has replaced eyes. c1940s. Courtesy Ross Schmidt.

Bi-Ba-Bo

piece weight poids par pièce, about environ 50 gr.

Monkey with white beard
Singe avec barbe blanche

mohair plush longh. No. 1312   *6.35*
peluche mohair, à p. long
cotton — coton   No. 1310

Bear — Ours

mohair plush, shorthaired
peluche mohair à poil court
No. 1300   *4.10*

mohair plush, longhaired
peluche mohair à poil long
No. 1301   *5.15*

King Charles
Chien King Charles

mohair plush, longhaired
peluche mohair à poil long
No. 1303   *6.—*

ILLUS. 171. This advertisement is for Bears, Monkeys and King Charles dogs. c1908.

made a Sooty (see **Sooty**) glove puppet.

Many Teddy Bear puppets are unmarked.

F.A.O. Schwarz of the USA advertised a "Freckle Face Bear" glove puppet in their 1938 catalogue at $1.50 each.

ILLUS. 173. English made glove puppet, tagged "Chiltern Hygienic Toys". 8in (20cm) long made from gold velvet plush. The head is filled with kapok, the eyes are glass. c1950s.

The Japanese soft-toy makers of the 1950s and 60s made several different types of Teddy Bear glove puppets. The Teddy Bear glove puppet is not as collectable as Teddy.

GRISLY

Founded in Germany in the small village of Kirchheimbolanden in 1954 by Karl Theodore Unfricht. Maker of soft toys, including Teddy Bears. The toys and Teddies can be made from synthetics and mohair.
Up until approximately 1975 the
62

ILLUS. 172. 22in (56cm) cream mohair Teddy Bear, fully jointed, glass eyes, black embroidered nose, mouth and claws. Tagged to the chest with a metal button depicting a bear standing on all fours together with the word "Grisly". c1950s. Courtesy Robyn Cox.

Grisly Teddy was tagged to the chest with a metal tag marked with the firm's trademark of a needle and thread superimposed on a bear standing on all fours. The metal tag has now been replaced by a paper tag.
Grisly Teddy Bears can be found in bright green and red as well as the traditional Teddy colours. Grisly Teddies are fully jointed and have broad shoulders.

GROWLER

Teddy Bears can make all sorts of sounds, squeaks, tinkles, music and growls. The growling Teddy is always popular and collectors of old Teddy Bears still become excited if a

ILLUS. 174. A self contained bakelite growler found in an Australian made Joy Toys Teddy c1938.

ILLUS. 175. A cardboard growler found in a German-made Teddy, from early 1900s. This growler contains a lead weight, bellow and whistle, the whole thing works on the tip-up principle forcing the lead weight to fall on the bellows and push wind through the whistle causing a growl-like noise.

ILLUS. 176. A very effective growler from the 1940s. Made of a cardboard cylinder with tin ends. The noise-making section is fixed to the inside end of the cylinder. It works on the tip-up principle causing the unfixed weighted end to push air through a noise maker.

ILLUS. 177. Taken at Goulburn in N.S.W . c1913.

lovely old bear can still growl.

Teddies have been fitted with growlers since they were first manufactured. An English mail-order catalogue from Faudels Ltd, London, 1912 advertises "Teddy Bear Growlers 2/-, 3/6, 3/9, 4/6, 5/6, 7/- each [20c, 35c, 38c, 45c, 55c, 70c] miniature 4/- dozen [40c]". A great deal of money in 1912.

Today the growler is a self-enclosed plastic cylinder that works on a tip-up principle emitting a life-like growl. However the early growlers were a very complex contraption of cardboard, wood, paper, lead weights, cloth and netting, all glued together and placed in Teddy's torso.

These early growlers also worked on a tip-up principle with a lead weight forcing air through cloth and wood bellows when the weight was shifted as Teddy was tipped over. It is little wonder that not many of these cardboard growlers of yesteryear can emit anything beside a dull "clunk" these days.

GUND

An old American toy company formed in 1889 by Adolph Gund. J. Swedlin, a partner in the company, bought the company in 1923, still retaining the founder's name, Gund. Makers of Teddies since the 1920s, Gund now manufacture the wonderful "Bialosky" range of bears. Winnie the Pooh bears (see **Winnie the Pooh**) are being manufactured by the Gund Company for the Sears stores in USA. The firm uses the slogan "Gotta Getta Gund".

ILLUS. 178. Gund advertisement c1984. Courtesy Australasian Sportsgoods and Toy Retailer.

64

ILLUS. 179. The beautiful Suzy by Gund from the Bialosky range of bears. She wears a woollen knitted dress and beret, is fully jointed, soft filled and made of the highest quality material.

ILLUS. 180. Bear and doll artist Anne Keane's Garrump. The elegant character in the book of the same name by Jim Picton-Warlow. Courtesy Anne Keane.

ABOVE LEFT

ILLUS. 181. A 12in (31cm) early Alpha Farnell Teddy.
Note his long feet. Fully jointed, kapok filled, oilcloth paw
pads. The shiny covering is lost on this little bear's pads
leaving a soft cotton pad that can very easily tear. This
Teddy has a particularly appealing expression. c1920s.

ABOVE RIGHT

ILLUS. 182. Two Alpha Farnell Teddies enjoy a ride on
their Steiff horse. The Teddies are fully jointed, kapok
filled, with brown glass eyes c1920s. The Steiff horse
wears a red saddle, he has shoe-button eyes and a white
horse hair mane and tail. The wheels are metal with
rubber tyres. Steiff button in the ear of the horse.

LEFT

ILLUS. 183. A trio of rare Alpha Farnell toys. The Teddies are 28in (71cm) tall and made from the highest
quality mohair, the Teddy standing has mohair plush
while the sitting Teddy has the long mohair. Both fully
jointed, the body and limbs are kapok filled while the head
and paws are excelsior filled. Oilcloth paw pads, the
features and claws are embroidered in fawn, they both
have beautiful quality large glass eyes. c1910. The doll
is tagged to the foot "Farnell's Alpha Toys - Made In
England". 16in (40cm) tall, the doll is fully jointed with a
cloth body and a felt head. Her hair is lengths of mohair
sewn on to the head, her features are moulded and
painted, she wears contemporary clothes c1920s.

ILLUS. 184. The Classic Toys' stand at the Sydney Toy Fair in 1971. Courtesy Australasian Sportsgoods and Toy Retailer.

ILLUS. 185. A publicity scene for L. J. Sterne's Humphrey B. Bear in 1966, featuring the toy Humphrey B. and the life size character Humphrey B. who is a very popular guest at children's functions. Courtesy L. J. Sterne.

HAND PUPPET
(see **Glove Puppet**)

HARRISON TEXTILES LTD
Makers of quality jointed and unjointed Teddy Bears first in Auckland, New Zealand, and now in Taiwan. The trademark is a doll hugging a Teddy Bear inside a heart - "Harrisons - Toys With Heart".
Produce a variety of Teddy Bears from 12in (30cm) to 32in (81cm) tall as well as dogs, ducks, swans and other soft toys.

ILLUS. 186. A group of Harrison Teddy Bears made in New Zealand c1983. Courtesy Australasian Sportsgoods and Toy Retailer.

HARWIN AND CO LTD
An English firm established in 1914 following the ban on German imports. Makers of soft toys including Teddy Bears and dolls. One of this firm's lines was the "Ally-Bear", these were fully jointed excelsior filled mohair Teddy Bears dressed in uniforms of the allies fighting in World War I. These included uniforms of soldiers, sailors, nurses, Russians, Generals and Captains. As the clothing of the Harwin Teddies is removable, certain identification of Harwin Teddy Bears is almost impossible. Harwin toys closely resemble those made by Steiff and were probably copied from Steiff.

HELVETIC
A Swiss firm, makers of beautiful quality Teddy Bears in the first quarter of 1900s including musical Teddies of colours other than traditional gold. In 1928 the trade magazine "Toy World" reported that Helvetic held the exclusive manufacturing rights of Teddy Bears with squeeze-operated music boxes. However other companies did manufacture this line of Teddy Bear. The Teddy Bears attributed to the Helvetic company are unmarked.

HERMANN, GEBR K G
A long established German toy - making company. This company began business in 1907 by Johann Hermann at Neufang near Sonneberg in Thuringia (in today's German Democratic Republic - GDR). From there the family was involved in Teddy Bear manufacturing until 1948 when Bernhard Hermann (the then head of the family) together with his three sons relocated the factory in Hirschaid near Bamberg in the American Zone of Germany (which is now the Fed-

1911 - 1929

1930 - 1939

1940 - 1951

1952 - 1989 on

ILLUS. 187. The Hermann trademark has changed little over the years.

RIGHT
ILLUS. 188. An early Teddy Bear c1910, probably by Hermann 25in (63.5cm) tall, fully jointed, shoe-button eyes, excelsior filled, black embroidered nose, mouth and claws. Courtesy Sotheby's Auctions, London.

67

LEFT
ILLUS. 189. A quality Harrison Teddy Bear. The blue
satin sash reads "I am a Growler Bear". Fully jointed
made from flame resistant plush. Made in New Zealand c1987.

RIGHT
ILLUS. 190. An all original and mint condition
Hermann Teddy c1952. Fully jointed, 16in
(41cm) tall, glass eyes, black embroided nose and
mouth, no claws. Gold mohair with peach coloured felt pads. Original blue bow and tag. The
tag reads "Hermann Teddy Original".

ILLUS. 192. Two all original Humphrey B. Bears, 24in (61cm) and 18in (46cm). Made in Australia by L.J. Sterne Doll Co.c1960.

ABOVE LEFT
ILLUS. 191. A Hermann Teddy Bear, 16in (41cm) tall, fully jointed, glass eyes, black embroidered nose, mouth and claws, excelsior filled. This Teddy is made from cotton plush, the paw pads from felt and the muzzle from mohair plush c1940s.

LEFT
ILLUS. 193. **Bookworm Bear.** This 30in (71cm) Merrythought Teddy Bear is enjoying a quiet moment with his old children's books, including the rare pop-up story books.

69

eral Republic of Germany).

The firm also underwent a name change at this time from Bernhard Hermann to Teddy Plüschspielwarenfabrik Gebr Hermann K G (Hermann Brothers Company, Manufacturers of Teddy Bears and plush toy animals).

The company has gone from strength to strength, producing the finest quality merchandise of wonderful design. The Hermann toy - making company uses "out - workers" extensively.

The company, although well known for its Teddy Bears, also produces a wide range of soft plush toy animals including leopards, panthers, lions, elephants, monkeys, birds of all types, dogs of all types, turtles, mice, crocodiles, whales, frogs etc. Baby toys have lately been added to the Hermann range.

The beautiful and very collectable Hermann Teddies are marked by a swing tag and do not carry a sewn-on label, making the identification of Hermann Teddies very difficult. However there are certain characteristics that can help with the identification. These include the company's preference for shaving the muzzle of some Teddies, although other companies also make Teddies with shaved muzzles.

Some early Hermann Teddies have very similar features to the Steiff Teddy, although the Hermann Teddies' features are not as exaggerated as the Steiff''s.

Included in the Hermann Teddy Bears being produced today are the Teddy Bears in the "Nostalgic" range. These include "Nostalgic Teddy Bears" in several sizes and types of fabric, "Nostalgic No-No Teddy Bear", "Nostalgic Teddy School" (see **Teddy Schools**) comprising six school desks and pupils, a teacher with his desk and two chalkboards.

Soft - filled unjointed, Pandas, Polar Bears and Teddies made in the bright colours of purple, red and blue are part of the range of modern Hermann Teddy Bears.

HOUSE OF NISBET LTD

An English firm of toy makers established in 1953 and acquired by Jack Wilson in 1975. The founder of the company is Peggy Nisbet, famous for her portrait collector dolls. The House of Nisbet specialises in producing quality collector dolls and bears, including the "Zodiac Bears" (see **Zodiac Bears**).

Other Teddy Bears produced by this company include:

The Bully Bears (see **Bully Bears**)
Delicatessen (see **Aloysius**)

Jack's Bears - made from distressed Alpaca fabric and advertised as "The Oldest New Bears in the World".

Signature Edition Bears. A series of Teddies sponsored by leading authors and artists. 12in (31cm) tall, each edition is limited to 5000 and each bear is signed by the sponsor. The Signature Edition series include the Michaud's Pearly King Bear, April Whitcomb's Clown Bear, Carol-Lynn Rossel Waugh's Yetta Bear, Rosemary Volpp's Anything Bear.

In May 1989 R. Dakin and Company acquired the share capital of House of Nisbet Ltd. Dakin's managing director in Europe, David Potter, assumed the role of managing director of House of Nisbet Ltd and Jack Wilson took on the post of director and honorary chairman.

House of Nisbet was strengthened both financially and commercially by joining forces with Dakin's European group, ready to compete in the highly competitive single European market in 1992.

HUGME BEARS
(see **Chiltern**)

HUMPHREY B. BEAR

An Australian character created in the early 1960s, and has featured in a children's television programme "Here's Humphrey" continuously since then. Dressed very distinctively in a checked vest and wearing a yellow tie and boater, Humphrey was first manufactured in Melbourne by soft toymaker L.J. Sterne until 1971. Humphrey is now made overseas and distributed by Classic Toys.

"Humphrey B. Bear" was initially made in two sizes of 18in (46cm) and 24in (61cm) in a synthetic plush, advertised as being "cuddly, lovable and safe, washable microfoam filled, socket fixed eyes and completely dressed with nothing to spend".

Humphrey was also made in a cut-and-sew version.

Many items are now made bearing Humphrey B. Bear's likeness.

ILLUS. 194. An 18in (46cm) cut and sew Humphrey B. Bear. The front is printed and the back is plain brown colour. Printed around the neck "Classic Toys Pty Ltd. Copyright Southern Television Comp Ltd 1965" Courtesy Marjory Fainges.

IDEAL TOY COMPANY

Formed in 1903 by a husband and wife team, Morris and Rose Michtom in New York City and then called the Ideal Novelty and Toy Company. Underwent a name change in 1938 to the present name, Ideal Toy Company.

The story goes that Morris Michtom, inspired by the 1902 Washington Post cartoon showing President Roosevelt's reluctance to shoot a bear cub, asked Rose to make a stuffed toy bear which was placed in the window of their small shop. The bear proved a success and the story goes that Mr Michtom then asked President Roosevelt for permission to call the toy bear "Teddy's Bear" - later to become Teddy Bear.

The first Teddy Bear made by Mrs Michtom was about 30in (76cm) tall and had shoe-button eyes. The earliest Ideal Teddies had a fabric nose rather than a stitched nose.

The company went from strength to strength producing Teddy Bears of imagination and quality. During the 1920s the Ideal Teddy became slimmer and novelty Teddies were produced in bright colours, including the Electric Eye Bear. At this time the company used the slogan "When we do it - we do it right".

In the 1930s the company began producing celebrity dolls, including the incredibly popular Shirley Temple dolls.

In the 1950s the United States government authorised the Ideal Toy Company to make Smokey the Bear (see **Smokey Bear**).

The company is still in existence today, making quality Teddy Bears and other toys.

ILLUS. 195.12 1/2in (32cm) Ideal Teddy Bear, unjointed, clip-in plastic eyes, vinyl nose. Brown synthetic fabric with contrasting lighter coloured feet and ears. Tagged to the leg seam "It's A Wonderful Toy It's Ideal. Made in USA by Ideal Toy Corp." c1950.

ILLUS. 196. This beautiful Teddy Bear is one of the first made by the Ideal Novelty Toy Company. It is on exhibition in the Smithsonian Institute, Washington, DC. Courtesy Smithsonian Institute.

ISRAELI TEDDY BEARS.

Dolls and soft toys including Teddy Bears have been manufactured in Israel since the 1960s, for the home market and for export.

RIGHT
ILLUS. 197. A 20in (51cm) Teddy Bear made of long synthetic plush with a velvet muzzle and paw pads. Plastic nose and eyes. Tagged in the arm seam "TOYLAND LTD.Contents all new material. Made in Israel". Courtesy Marjory Fainges.

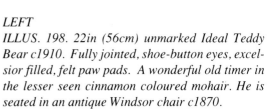

LEFT
ILLUS. 198. 22in (56cm) unmarked Ideal Teddy Bear c1910. Fully jointed, shoe-button eyes, excelsior filled, felt paw pads. A wonderful old timer in the lesser seen cinnamon coloured mohair. He is seated in an antique Windsor chair c1870.

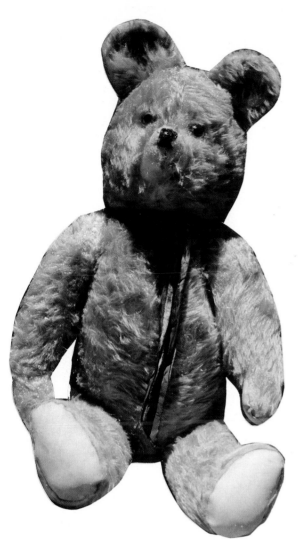

ILLUS. 199. A rare 27 1/2in (70cm) tall early Jakas Teddy Bear. Jointed limbs, mohair fabric, glass eyes and stiff neck. Tagged on the left foot seam "Jakas Toys Regd Design No 37660". Courtesy Obie Bronte.

ILLUS. 200. **Teddies look good anywhere.** An early American kitchen dresser makes an ideal display case. The top shelf features a rare collection of Easter carton candy containers in the form of rabbits and chickens. On the second shelf, six early Teddies look right at home. The lower shelf holds a collection of dolls in American Indian costumes, all from the first quarter of the century. Courtesy Susan Weiser.

ILLUS. 201. **Australian Made.** The Teddy on the left is a 24in (61cm) Joy Toys Teddy Bear c1950. Beautiful quality long mohair fabric, jointed limbs, glass eyes, rubber filled. The blocks were made by Ruth Floth, the Teddy on the right is Wilbur by Debra Aldridge. Fully jointed with glass eyes, plush fabric. Wilbur wears a little red waistcoat. The tiny Teddy is Robearn Hood, by Marjory Fainges.

73

ILLUS. 202. c1940. Courtesy N.S.W. State Library.

JACKIE

Jackie, the Jubilee Teddy, is a Teddy Bear released in 1953 by Steiff (see **Steiff**) to commemorate 50 years of Teddy making. Re-released in 1978. The Jackie Teddy is fully jointed, has a rounded fat torso and short limbs. The feet have four claws on each paw. The distinctive thing about the Jackie Teddy Bear is a horizontal white stitch on the black vertical stitched nose.

ILLUS. 203. The Steiff "Jackie" featured in the 1960 Dare Wright picture-story book. (see Storybook Bears).

JACK'S BEAR
(see **House of Nisbet**)

JAKAS PTY LTD

Commenced business in 1954, in Melbourne, Australia, making soft toys, including Teddy Bears. The original Teddies were fully jointed but the style changed within a very short time to the unjointed type of Teddy that is still made today.

Jakas Teddies are guaranteed to be washable and carry a tag stating so. Each one is hand finished.

The most famous Jakas Teddy is Big Ted, the Teddy that entertains children via the ABC television programme "Playschool".

Jakas Teddies are made in several sizes and colours. Pandas and Koalas are also in the Jakas range of toys.

ABOVE
ILLUS. 204. Three 13in (33cm) Jakas Teddy Bears. Unjointed, machine washable, safety clip-in eyes. Tagged to the left foot "Jakas Toys Med.Wash in luke warm Lux". Courtesy Marjory Fainges.

JAPANESE

From the 1920s the Japanese-made Teddies could be found on most markets, including Europe, UK, USA and Australia. These cheap imports soon proved very popular. The Teddies were exported worldwide during the 1960s and 1970s. Features of Japanese-made Teddies include wire joints, synthetic fabric, little or no shaping to limbs, mostly excelsior filled. Most Japanese Teddies are not tagged.

JANUS
(see **Schuco**)

JOCKLINE
(see **Avanti**)

ILLUS. 205. A 24in (61cm) Japanese made Teddy Bear. Fully jointed, excelsior filled. Made from frosted synthetic fabric with felt paw pads and inner ears. Very unstable wire joints c1960s.

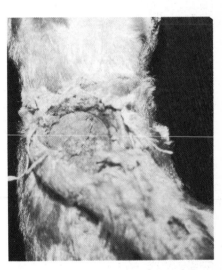

ILLUS. 206. This Teddy Bear is jointed with metal discs that have gone rusty and damaged the fabric of the arm, English Teddy Bear c1930s.

JOINTS

Most Teddy Bears have five joints, enabling the arms, legs and head to move. This type of Teddy is known as "fully jointed".

Some Teddies can have the limbs jointed but not the head. Australian manufacturers of Teddies favoured this type of jointing. These Teddies are referred to as "stiff-necked Teddies". Another method of jointing is the arms only, with the head, torso and legs made in one piece. This type

ILLUS. 207. During the koalamania of the 1930s koala teacosies were very popular. This rare teacosy is made from kangaroo skin, and lined with quilted satin. The head and arms of the koala are cork filled. The koala pouch holds a joey egg-warmer. It is also lined with quilted satin, shoe-button eyes and cork filled head. The baby joey has no arms.

LEFT
ILLUS. 208. A Joy Toys doll holds a koala decorated muff. The doll is 30in (76cm) tall, flock filled, made of felt with a pressed cotton face. Tiny mohair curls peep from the brim of the bonnet. The muff is kangaroo skin, the koala head is cork filled with shoe-button eyes. A purse is concealed inside the muff. Both the doll and muff are c1930.

ILLUS. 209. A hug of beautiful Teddies. From left to right 22in (56cm) unusual bright gold colour Merrythought, fully jointed, luxuriant long mohair. Glass eyes, c1948. The next Teddy is a Chad Valley bear. Always a favourite with collectors is this next little Teddy, a 14in (36cm) Merrythought Cheeky with a velvet muzzle, bells in his ears and wrap-around claws. A 28in (71cm) big boy Merrythought Teddy is next, c1946, and then a tagged baby Merrythought Teddy, 14in (36cm) tall with rather high shoulders that give him a very distinctive look, c1956. The four Merrythought Teddy Bears are of the highest quality, they are all fully jointed and filled with kapok.

ILLUS. 210. *Two beautiful Steiff koalas. Harder to find than cousin Teddy, c1950s. Fully jointed, long mohair fabric with plush paws and faces and a felt nose. Courtesy David Worland.*

ILLUS. 211. ***A game of cricket anyone!*** *These two wonderful koala cricketers were made by Joyce Patterson of Ballarat in Victoria. Made of grey velour with the ears, moustache and beard made from long synthetic fur fabric. The clothes are removable and the bats are hand whittled. Superb examples of a modern collectable.*

LEFT
ILLUS. 215. This 16in (41cm) tall Japanese made Teddy was made in the 1940s. Fully jointed, dense synthetic plush, large glass eyes. The muzzle and paw pads are made from contrasting white velvet material. The claws are drawn on the front paws and the claws and pads are drawn on the boot-like feet. This unusual and crude marking is original. Note the joints are external and not internal.

of jointing is usually used as a cost-saving method.

Teddies can also be found with the torso and limbs unjointed and only the head jointed.

Today many Teddies are made with plastic clip-in joints; however, the usual type of joints in use before the advent of the modern clip-in were the wooden disc-type joints comprising two wooden discs, two metal washers and a metal pin.

Some firms used cardboard or compressed fibre discs instead of wood. This type of joint can collapse if Teddy is exposed to damp or he suffers a dunking. Metal discs have also been used and again if Teddy has ever been wet or exposed to damp, the metal discs will rust and can damage Teddy's fabric.

Japanese manufacturers favoured the use of wire joints; much cheaper than the disc method. The heavy gauge wire passed from the limb into torso and the end was bent over to hold it in position. The wire often breaks through the material causing the loss of a limb.

The well-made Teddy of yesteryear can still be found firmly jointed after many years of service; however, many more poorly made Teddy Bears can now be found suffering from wobbly heads and dangling limbs and perhaps corrective surgery should be used on these problems before more damage is done by the loose joint perhaps causing the fabric to tear and making repairs almost impossible.

JOY TOYS

An Australian company, probably the first to mass-produce Teddy Bears in Australia. The company began business in South Yarra, Victoria, in the early 1920s. The original owners of Joy Toys, Mr & Mrs Kirby, moved

ILLUS. 213. The Joy Toys logo.

ILLUS. 214. A Joy Toys tag found on a 10in (25cm) Teddy. This tag is sewn around the bottom of the leg, as the foot is too small for the tag.

ILLUS. 216. This tag is sewn into the foot seam of the later 1960 Joy Toys Teddy.

ILLUS. 217. Sewn on to the oil cloth paw pad of a 1940s Teddy.

production to a larger factory in 1930. In 1937 Mr M. Court took over the company and reconstructed it. Joy Toys boomed and an estimated 50,000 Teddies were sold during the firm's existence.

Over 150 different soft toys were manufactured by Joy Toys, including Snow White and the Seven Dwarves made under franchise from Walt Disney. Made in fabric, these quality toys soon lost their popularity when the film of that name had finished playing and as not many were made they are now considered rare collector items.

The very first Joy Toys Teddies were fully jointed; however, very quickly they were made without a neck joint - a peculiarity of most Australian-made Teddies, even of the better quality ones.

Joy Toys were tagged on the foot - "Joy Toys Made in Australia"; however a little Teddy of just 10in (25cm) had his tag sewn vertically up his leg. Pre 1940 Joy Toy Teddies had felt paw pads. After that painted "leatherette" was used, but the paint would lift on some paw pads exposing the cotton backing. Often this softer material will split causing loss of the filling.

Early Joy Toys Teddies from the 1920s were excelsior filled. Then in the 1930s flock and kapok were used in the main with excelsior used in paws and noses. In the 1940s and 1950s crumbed rubber was used. This material breaks down very easily if not stored correctly and consequently many Joy Toys Teddies from this era suffer from lumpy limbs and torso!

Initially, 100% mohair fabric was used in production. When this became too expensive, a mohair and synthetic mix fabric was used until, in the late 1960s, a fully synthetic fabric resembling brushed cotton was introduced.

Most Australian-made Teddies have several distinguishing features. These are shared by the Joy Toys Teddies. Beside the stiff necks, the front paws are slightly pointed and upturned. Joy Toys Teddies' ears are of a large size and the nose of a black

vertical thread has the extreme outside stitches longer than the rest.

By the early 1960s the company could not compete with cheap imports and in 1963 Cyclops bought the company. Toltoys now own the name Joy Toys and it was last used in 1976.

JUBILEE TEDDY
(see **Jackie**)

ILLUS. 218. This 30in (76cm) Joy Toys Teddy Bear is jointed only at the neck. The clothing is incorporated into the body structure, the top is velvet plush, the pants and paw pads are felt, while the head is mohair and features the distinctive nose shape of a Joy Toys Teddy, and beautiful glass eyes. Perhaps made during the war years of 1939-1945 when most fabric beside felt was unobtainable for the Australian toy industry. Courtesy Patricia Maiden.

ILLUS. 219. Two Joy Toys Teddies. That on the left is fully jointed 14in (36cm) tall. This is the earliest type of Joy Toys, and quite rare. He is excelsior filled, mohair fabric with cloth paw pads. The nose has the distinctive outer stitches larger than the rest of the nose c1930s. The little fellow behind him is c1950s. He has a stiff neck and is kapok filled with excelsior in the muzzle. He has lost his original eyes. Tagged to the left foot "Joy-Toys - Made in Australia". Courtesy Debra Aldridge.

79

ILLUS. 220. **A bear and his jig-saw.** This beautiful 25in (40cm) Teddy Bear is fully jointed, excelsior filled and made from the highest quality mohair. His paw pads are felt, his nose, mouth and claws are embroidered in fawn. This special Teddy has "electric eyes". A battery is sewn into the back of Teddy's head and the eyes are operated by pressing an ear under the left ear. Maker unknown, c1920s. The jig-saw puzzle is called "Teddy Bear Capers - Junior Jigs". Made by Bell of England. The box contains two jig-saw puzzles, box is marked two shillings and six pence and is c1950.

ILLUS. 221. February 1971. Courtesy Australasian Sportsgoods and Toy Retailer.

ILLUS. 222. A later Joy Toys Teddy c1960s. This 16in (41cm) attractive Teddy is made of brushed cotton with brown felt paw pads, jointed limbs and a stiff neck. Even at this late date the firm was still using beautiful glass eyes. Tagged to the right foot "Joy-Toys - Made in Australia".

ILLUS. 223. Big is beautiful! This 26in (66cm) Teddy Bear is a 1940s Joy Toys. Tagged to the left foot "Joy Toys - Made in Australia". He has the typical stiff neck of a Joy Toys bear, quality mohair fabric with oil cloth paw pads. His eyes are replacements. Many Joy Toys Teddy Bears are found with replaced eyes.

ILLUS. 226. In 1971 the Joy Toys Teddy was advertised as made from mohair "with swivelled arms and legs". Courtesy Australasian Sportsgoods and Toy Retailer.

ILLUS. 224. A very sweet little Joy Toys Teddy. Jointed limbs with a stiff neck, quality mohair fabric, felt paw pads, glass eyes. Tagged to the right foot. c1940s.

RIGHT
ILLUS. 225. 16in (41cm) Joy Toys Teddy. Tagged to the right foot, long mohair, oil-cloth paw pads, jointed limbs with a stiff neck. Note the beautiful large glass eyes.

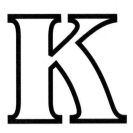

K

KAHN AND MOSSBACHER
(see **Clothes**)

KAPOK
Over the years English and Australian soft-toy makers have favoured the use of kapok as a filling (see **Filling**). Kapok is a silky white vegetable fibre from the fruit pods of the White Silk Cotton Tree.

KATHE KRUSE
A German firm more famous for beautiful cloth dolls and now plastic and cloth dolls. Makes unjointed Teddies from synthetic plush, filled with foam rubber.

KERSA
A German made Teddy, pre World War II, fully jointed, quality mohair, glass eyes, metal tag on both feet "Kersa - Made in Germany".

KNICKERBOCKER TOY COMPANY LTD
This long-established toy-making firm was situated in New York State, USA, and manufactured soft toys and Teddy Bears since the early 1900s.
The quality Knickerbocker Teddy has a distinctive separately sewn-in muzzle and paw pads and is tagged in the centre seam in the front of the torso. Large ears are also a feature of a Knickerbocker Teddy.
During the 1960s this firm manufactured Smokey Bears (see **Smokey Bear**).
Always a quality product, the now nonexistent Knickerbocker Toy Company used the slogan "Toys of Distinction".

ILLUS. 228. 20in (51cm) tall brown bear fully jointed, long mohair with velveteen paw pads, glass eyes, soft filled torso with hard filled head. Not tagged but thought to be a 1940s Knickerbocker Teddy. Courtesy Susan Weiser.

ILLUS. 227. Puss in Boots is 16in (41cm) tall, fully jointed and is thought to be made by the German firm of Kersa. Fully jointed, black plush with red felt boots. Inner ears are black felt.

ILLUS. 229. 21in (53cm) Knickerbocker Teddy with cardboard innersoles on his large feet that enable him to stand unaided. Shaved muzzle with open mouth and the turned down paws give this special Teddy a baby like appearance c1940. Courtesy L. Albright.

83

KNITTED

Knitted Teddies have always been popular, perhaps if there hasn't been money to buy a Teddy then a knitted one, even from recycled wool, would be just as welcome.

"Large Teddy Bear 1934"

Directions for making a really large bear. They are very expensive indeed to buy, and are as easy to knit at home as an ordinary jumper or other garment. Or if this Teddy is knitted on finer needles with finer wool the size of the toy will be smaller accordingly.

Materials - 1lb 6oz of brown wool, 1 1/2oz of light fawn wool, one pair of bone knitting needles size 8, two large pearl buttons for eyes, black wool for marking face and claws, 1 1/4 yards of ribbon for neck, and 2 yards of unbleached calico.

Measurements - Height, 29ins, width round body, 33ins.

Tension - 5 stitches to 1in in width, and 9 rows to 1in in depth, after pressing.

The Body

This is worked in two halves. Begin at the bottom of the front. Cast on 12 stitches and knit 3 rows plain.

4th row: Increase 1 in first stitch, knit to end (13)

Knit 5 rows on 13 stitches.

Work on principle of last 6 rows 3 times more (16) then knit 16 rows on these stitches.

44th row: Increase 1 in first stitch, knit to end (17)

Knit 9 rows on 17 stitches.

54th row: Increase 1 in first stitch, knit to end (18), then knit 3 rows on 18 stitches.

Work on principle of last 4 rows 5 times more (23).

78th row: Increase 1 in first stitch, knit to end (24)

79th row: Knit 24

Work on principle of last 2 rows 3 times more (27)

86th row: Increase 1 in first stitch, knit to end (28)

87th row: Increase 1 in last stitch (29)

Work on principle of last 2 rows 4 times more (37)

96th row: Cast on 50, knit to end (87), then knit 77 rows on 87 stitches.

174th row: Knit 39, put the remaining 48 stitches on a safety-pin for front of body and shoulder. You will now work the back part only.

175th row: Knit 2 tog. at beginning, knit to end (38)

176th row: Knit 38.

Work on principle of last 2 rows twice more (36) then knit 4 more rows on 36 stitches.

185th row: Knit 2 tog. at beginning, knit to end (35), then knit 3 rows on 35 stitches.

Work on principle of last 4 rows 4 times more (31), then knit 20 rows on 31 stitches.

225th row: Knit 2 tog. at beginning, knit to end (30).

226th row: Knit last 2 stitches tog. (29).

Work on principle of last 2 rows 3 times more (23).

233rd row: Cast off all but 12 stitches. Put these on a safety-pin for the back of head.

174th row of front: Pick up the stitches from the first safety-pin, joining wool to middle of body, and cast off 10 stitches for the armhole. Knit to end (38).

175th row: Knit last 2 stitches tog (37)

176th row: Knit 2 tog. at beginning, knit to end (36)

Work on principle of last 2 rows 3 times more (30)

183rd row: Knit last 2 stitches tog. (29), then knit 3 rows on 29 stitches.

Work on principle of last 4 rows once (28), then knit 14 rows on 192 stitches.

205th row: Knit 2 tog. at beginning, knit to end (27), then knit 3 rows on 27 stitches.

Work on principle of last 4 rows once (26), then knit 6 rows on 26 stitches.

219th row: Knit 2 tog. at beginning, and increase 1 in last stitch, then knit 3 rows on 26 stitches.

Repeat these 4 rows 5 times.

243rd row: Cast off 9 stitches, increasing 1 in last stitch (18)

244th row: Knit last 2 tog. (17)

245th row: Knit 2 tog. at beginning, increase 1 in last stitch.

Work on principle of last 2 rows twice more (15)

250th row: Knit 2 tog. at each end (13)

Repeat this row 6 times, break off the wool.

Pick up 39 stitches of the 50 cast on, nearest to the outside edge. Join the wool to the end nearest the middle of body.

1st row: Knit 2 tog. at beginning, knit to end (38)

2nd row: Knit last 2 tog. (37)

Work on principle of last 2 rows 8 times more (21), then knit 4 rows on 21 stitches.

23rd row: Knit 2 tog. at beginning, knit to end (20), then knit 3 rows on 20 stitches.

Work on principle of last 4 rows 3 times more (17),then knit 6 rows on 17 stitches.

45th row: Knit 2 tog. at beginning, knit to end (16), then knit 3 rows on 16 stitches.

49th row: Knit 2 tog. at each end (14) then knit 3 rows on 14 stitches.

Work on principle of last 4 rows once more (12), then knit 6 rows on 12 stitches.

63rd row: Knit 2 tog. at each end (10), then knit 2 rows on 10 stitches and cast off.

Knit another piece in exactly the same way. Sew the two pieces together down the back, leaving about 6 inches.Open at the bottom for stuffing. Now pick up the 24 stitches from the safety-pin (12 stitches on each piece of knitting) that were left for the back of head and knit 2 rows.

3rd row: Increase 1 at each end (26), then knit 3 rows on 26 stitches.

Work on principle of last 4 rows twice more (30).

15th row: Increase 1 at each end (32), then knit 5 rows on 32 stitches.

Work on principle of last 6 rows twice more (36).

33rd row: Increase 1 at each end (38), then knit 3 rows on 38 stitches.

Work on principle of last 4 rows 5 times more (48).

57th row: Increase 1 at each end (50), then knit 29 rows on 50 stitches.

87th row: Knit 2 tog. at each end (48), then knit 3 rows on 48 stitches.

Work on principle of last 4 rows 5 times more (38).

111th row: Knit 2 tog. at each end (36)

112th row: Knit 36.

Work on principle of last 2 rows 7 times more (22), then knit 10 rows on 22 stitches.

137th row: Knit 2 tog. at each end (20), then knit 3 rows on 20 stitches.

Work on principle of last 4 rows once more (18)..

145th row: Knit 2 tog. at each end (16)

146th row: Knit 16

Work on principle of last 2 rows once more (14)

149th row: Knit 2 tog. at each end (12)

Repeat this row 3 times (6), then cast off.

The Face

Begin at the front neck. Cast on 38 stitches and knit 4 rows.

5th row: Increase 1 at each end (40), then knit 3 rows on 40 stitches

Work on principle of last 4 rows twice more (44).

17th row: Increase 1 in first stitch, knit to end (45).

18th row: Knit 45.

19th row: Increase 1 at each end of the needle (47)

20th row: Knit 47

Work on principle of last 4 rows 3 times more (53)

33rd row: Cast on 8 stitches for nose, knit to end (61)

34th row: Knit 61

35th row: Increase 1 at each end (63), then knit 21 rows on 63 stitches.

57th row: Knit last 2 tog. (62), then knit 3 rows on 62 stitches.

Work on principle of last 4 rows twice more (60)

69th row: Cast off 23, knit 2 tog at each end (35)

70th row: Knit 35.

71st row: Knit 2 tog. at each end (33)

72nd row: Knit 33

Work on principle of last 2 rows 3 times more (27)

79th row: Knit 2 tog. at each end (25)

Repeat this last row 7 times (11), then cast off.

Knit another piece in exactly the same way.

The Ears

Begin at the bottom.

Cast 44 stitches and knit 2 rows.

3rd row: Knit 2 tog. at each end (42), then knit 3 rows on 42 stitches.

Work on principle of last 4 rows 3 times more (36)

19th row: Knit 2 tog. at each end (34)

20th row: Knit 34

Work on principle of last 2 rows 5 times more (24)

31st row: Knit 2 tog. at beginning, middle and end (21)

Repeat this row 6 times, leaving 3, then cast off.

Knit another ear in exactly the same way.

The Forelegs

Begin at the bottom.

Cast on 12 stitches and knit 2 rows.

3rd row: Increase 1 at each end (14)

4th row: Knit 14

Work on principle of last 2 rows twice more (18)

9th row: Increase 1 in first stitch (19)

10th row: Knit 19

Work on principle of last 2 rows 3 times more (22), then knit 12 rows on 22 stitches.

29th row: Knit 2 tog. at beginning, (21), then knit 3 rows on 21 stitches.

Work on principle of last 4 rows twice more (19)

41st row: Increase 1 in first stitch (20)

42nd row: Cast on 20 stitches, knit to end (40)

43rd row: Increase 1 at each end of the needle (42), then knit 3 rows on 42 stitches.

Work on principle of last 4 rows 24 times more (90)

143rd row: Knit 2 tog twice at the beginning of row, knit 58, cast off 18 stitches, knit the remaining stitches, cast off.

Now join wool to where you began casting off the 18 stitches, knit to end of the row (60)

144th row: Knit 2 tog. at each end of the needle (58)

145th row: Knit

Work on principle of last 2 rows 10 times more (38)

166th row: Knit 2 tog. at each end (36)

Repeat this row 5 times (26), then cast off.

For inside of hand pick up the 20 cast-on stitches in the 42nd row, using fawn wool.

1st row: Increase 1 at beginning (21), then knit 3 rows on 21 stitches.

Work on principle of last 4 rows once more (22), then knit 14 rows on 22 stitches.

23rd row: Knit 2 tog. at beginning (21)

24th row: Knit 21

Work on principle of last 2 rows 3 times more (18)

31st row: Knit 2 tog. at each end (16).

32nd row: Knit 16

Work on principle of last 2 rows twice more (12), then cast off. Work another leg in the same way.

The Hind Legs

Begin at the bottom.

Cast on 94 stitches and knit 28 rows.

29th row: Knit 2 tog. at each end (92), then knit 5 rows on 92 stitches.

Work on principle of last 6 rows once more (90)

41st row: Knit 2 tog. at each end (88)

Repeat this row 5 times more (78)

47th row: Knit 2 tog. twice at each end (74)

Repeat this row once (70), then knit 8 rows on 70 stitches.

57th row: Increase 1 at each end (72), then knit 5 rows.

Work on principle of last 6 rows 6 times more (84)

99th row: Increase 1 in first stitch, knit 12 more stitches, and slip these on to a cotton (14 in all), cast off 4, knit 2 tog., knit to the end of row, increasing 1 in last stitch.

100th row: Knit on last 68

101st row: Knit 2 tog. at beginning (67)

102nd row: Knit 67

Work on principle of last 2 rows twice more (65)

107th row: Knit 2 tog. at beginning, increase 1 in last stitch.

108th row: Knit 65
109th row: Knit 2 tog. at beginning (64)
Knit another piece in exactly the same way.

The Soles
With light fawn wool cast on 10 stitches and knit 1 row.
2nd row: Increase 1 at each end (12)
3rd row: Knit 12
Work on principle of last 2 rows 5 times more (22), then knit 34 rows on 22 stitches.
48th row: Knit 2 tog. at each end (20)
49th row: Knit 20
Work on principle of last 2 rows 5 times more (10), and cast off.
Knit another sole in exactly the same way.

To Make Up
Brush up all the parts (except the soles and inside of hands) well with a wire brush. Cut out all the parts in strong calico lining, allowing 3/4in for the making up and tack well all round the edges and across the limbs, leaving all the tacking threads in white after the animal is stuffed. When making up sew all the knitted parts together with wool, then whip the calico over with strong cotton. Join the body up the front, sew the side of the head to the head-piece. Sew the nose together and along the throat. Sew up the forelegs, then sew to the body, place the seam 5 inches from the shoulder seam. Join up the hind legs and sew on the soles. Cut a piece of cardboard the same shape and place this in each foot. This keeps the soles flat when stuffed. Sew in the legs, placing the seam 9 inches from the seam in front of the body. Stuff well with kapok down, flock or anything light suitable for stuffing. Sew up the opening at the back that was left for the stuffing. Take out all the tacking threads. Sew on the ears, mark the nose, mouth and claws with black wool, sew in the eyes. To make these get two large pearl buttons, marking the pupils with black Indian ink. Paint all round them with red water-colour paint, when perfectly dry paint over with clear varnish or glue. Smooth the animal down with a wire brush and tie the ribbon round his neck. Stiffen outer edges of ears with wire.

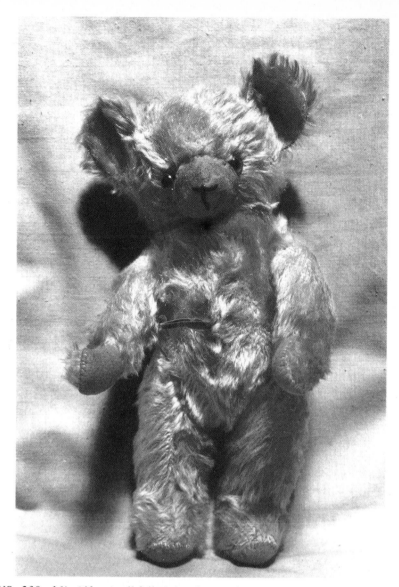

ILLUS. 230. 16in (41cm) tall fully jointed very sweet Knickerbocker Teddy. Large glass eyes, felt muzzle and paw pads, good quality mohair. Tagged to the torso centre seam, soft filled torso with hard filled head. Press squeaker in the torso c1950.

ILLUS. 231. The tag in the torso centre seam of the 1950s Knickerbocker Teddy is white cloth with blue writing "Knickerbocker Toy Co Inc. Another toy of distinction". The tag is very fragile and placed in such a vulnerable position in the middle of Teddy's tummy it is a wonder it still remains after all these years.

If an upright model is desired, knit in exactly the same way, but place the seams of the legs 6 inches from the seam in front of the body. This makes a model 39 inches high.

KOALA BEARS

Koala - an Aboriginal word meaning an animal that can live without drinking water.

A cousin to Teddy, the koala is also enjoying a new lease of life as a toy since the early 1980s.

To the everlasting shame of Australia, the first toy koalas were made from koala skins. These toys were fully jointed with leather noses and claws, shoe-button eyes and were cork filled. A law passed by Parliament in 1930 prohibited the killing or keeping of koalas, resulting in "Koalamania". By the early 1930s toy koalas were made from kangaroo skin. Again the first examples had leather noses and claws, shoe-button eyes and were cork filled. Kangaroo skin is still in use. The very early

ILLUS. 233. A Teddy-koala made of leather, fully jointed, excelsior filled, beautiful big blue glass eyes. c1920. A rare combination of a Teddy Bear and a koala. Courtesy Marjory Fainges.

ILLUS. 232. Novel koala money box. Note the reference to the USA Servicemen, in Australia for Rest and Recreation leave from Vietnam in 1968. Courtesy Australasian Sportsgoods and Toy Retailer.

LEFT
ILLUS. 234. The 1920s Teddy-koala showing the body shape.

ILLUS. 235. August 1963. Courtesy Australasian Sportsgoods and Toy Retailer.

ILLUS. 236. Ready for the tourist trade. A selection of Koalas, all unjointed with glass eyes, moulded plastic nose and claws. c1986. Courtesy Blue Shield Marketing Pty Ltd.

koalas were jointed, but by the mid 1930s the body and limbs were made in one piece as they are today. In the 1940s the noses and claws were made from rubber, the eyes were made from glass. Plastic has been used since the late 1950s, for claws and noses and is still in use today. Many koala decorated items were made during the "Koalamania" period. These included kangaroo-skin products such as purses, handbags, muffs, tea-cosies and nightdress and pyjama cases all decorated with little koalas.

Bookends, vases, ornaments, fire screens, etc were all made decorated with koalas in one form or another.

Today, kangaroo-skin toy koalas are still very popular with tourists. However, soft-filled cute little koalas made from washable synthetic fabric are now popular as children's toys.

Wonderful character koalas have emerged over the years. They include Blinky Bill and Billy Blue Gum (see **Blinky Bill** see **Billy Blue Gum**).

88

L

LAUGHING TEDDIES

Laughing Teddy Bears are Teddies made with open mouths, and they were made by most manufacturers at some time. However the Columbia Teddy Bear Manufacturers (see **Columbian Teddy Bear Manufacturers**) of USA did manufac-ture probably the

ILLUS. 237.
A baby bear, maker unknown. Fully jointed, synthetic plush fabric with fawn felt paw pads and inner mouth. Beautiful big glass eyes, three claws on each paw. The front paws are turned down, the feet have cardboard inner soles.

original Laughing Teddy Bear in 1908. This Teddy had a wide open mouth showing two rows of gleaming white teeth and, according to the American trade magazine "Play-things" of 1908, "is being well received throughout the trade". Another wonderful example of a laughing Teddy is the Peter Bear (see Peter Bear). This rare Teddy was made in Germany and also has two rows of teeth showing in his wide open mouth.

Many firms made open-mouth Teddies, including the German firms of Steiff and Hermann. The Steiff company has made many open-mouth Teddies and it would appear this happy fellow is a favourite with this firm.

Some of the Steiff open-mouth Teddies include:

1930 Bear Doll, only head and paws are mohair, the body is dressed.
1950 Orsini, sitting, unjointed.
1957 Floppy Zotty soft filled, lies on tummy, unjointed.
1957 Teddy Baby fully jointed, can stand on two legs unaided.
1960 Minky Zotty imitation fur, jointed.
1960 Panda, jointed.
1969 Hand puppet.
1970 Cosy Teddy dralon, jointed.
1975 Fristed pull string talking bear.
1977 Zooby standing, unjointed.
1980 Lully unjointed.
1980 Cosy Orsi standing on all fours, unjointed.

The Hermann Company has also produced many beautiful open-mouth laughing Teddies in frosted mohair with velvet muzzles and turned-down paws, known as Zotty. (see **Zotty**)

Other open-mouth bears were made by "Heunec" of Germany; a pull-string talking bear with long frosted mohair, c1950s. Eli of Germany made a fully jointed open-mouth Teddy during the 1950s. Many beautiful open-mouth laughing Teddies are unmarked but English, German and Japanese companies all produced

ILLUS. 238. This unusual laughing Teddy Bear was won in a "Bear Milk" competition. Fully jointed, red claws and inner mouth. A very large head for the size of the body. Courtesy Wendy Benson.

these lovable popular laughing Teddy Bears.

ILLUS. 239. This happy little laughing Teddy Bear is made from beaver-lamb skin with red leather paw pads and inner mouth. Fully jointed, with a moulded rubber nose, excelsior filled, c1940.

ILLUS. 240. December 1963, Courtesy Australasian Sportsgoods and Toy Retailer.

The Prestige Name in Soft Toys

ILLUS. 241. The attractive Lindee trademark.

ILLUS. 242.The Lindee tag. Made from white satin -like material with the logo of the reclining fawn and "Lindee Toys Made In Australia" printed in red.

ILLUS. 243. 1969 Courtesy Australasian Sportsgoods and Toy Retailer.

90

LEFT
ILLUS. 244. A wonderful Lindee Teddy Bear. Long quality mohair fabric, oil cloth paw pads, fully jointed, large glass eyes. The embroidered nose, mouth and claws are very large and give this 14in (36cm) Teddy a very appealing quality, c1948.

LINDEE

An Australian company now out of production.

Situated in Sydney, NSW, this firm produced quality Teddy Bears, pandas, dolls and other soft toys from 1944 to 1976. Tagged to the foot with a cloth tag bearing the figure of a reclining fawn together with the words, "Lindee Toys - Made in Australia". Several different types of Teddies were produced, the earlier ones made before 1960 were made from imported mohair plush, fully jointed with glass eyes. One type had a moulded plastic nose.

This firm won the "Toy of the Year" award in Australia in 1969.

RIGHT
ILLUS. 245. A later Lindee Teddy Bear. 20in (51cm) tall, fully jointed . Made from a synthetic plush with vinyl paw pads. Large glass eyes, moulded plastic nose. This Teddy still has his label on the paw pad seam, c1965.

ILLUS. 246. Baby Elaine Ann Shinner was one year old in 1969 when she was given her beautiful Lindee panda. Photo courtesy Myrtle Parker.

LEFT
ILLUS. 247. These two Schuco mechanical roller-skate Teddies were made approximately thirty years apart. The bear on the left is 8in (20cm) tall with glass eyes, fully jointed, mohair fabric with felt paw pads. His skates have rubber wheels. He is tagged "Made In U.S. Zone Schuco-Rolly-Germany" c1950. The bear on the right is also 8in (20cm) tall, he has shoe-button eyes, mohair fabric, he is dressed in his original yellow jacket and brown pants. His skates are metal, the wheels are tin, c1920. Both Teddies have propelling sticks and are key wind. The key is in the back of each bear. Courtesy Marvin Cohen Auctions.

M

MALROB

Manufactured unjointed Teddy Bears in Brisbane, Australia, from 1961 until 1985.

The Teddy Bears are made from synthetic fabric in sizes 10in (25.4cm) to 60in (152.4cm). The eyes and the moulded nose is plastic. The Teddy is made in a variety of colours, including gold, blue and pink. The tag on the side of the leg reads "Malrob Cuddle Toys, Made in Australia".

Malrob also manufactured Panda Bears and soft toys.

MATERIALS

Teddy Bears have been made from almost every conceivable type of material, including woven fabric (see **Fabric**).

Materials used over the years include gold, silver, porcelain, bisque, tin, wood, rubber, paper, papier-mache, celluloid, glass, plastic and vinyl.

Since early this century Teddy Bear charms have been made from gold. Charms, baby rattles, jewellery and seals have been made from hall-marked sterling silver and silverplate. A Grace Brothers, Sydney, catalogue 1911, advertises a sterling silver "Teddy" Tie Pin for 1/- [10c].

German jointed bisque Teddies usually in small sizes have been manufactured since early 1900s. Schuco miniature bears are made from fabric-covered tin (see **Schuco**).

Battery-driven bears are made from a combination of tin and fabric (see **Battery**).

For many years bears have been carved from wood. The Germans made particularly beautiful examples of carved bears on hall stands, lamp stands, table bases, clocks, etc. which were very popular from the beginning of 1900 until the 1930s.

Several examples of rubber squeaker

ILLUS. 248. A fine example of carved wooden bears. Approximately 4ft (1.2m) tall. These bears are part of a two branch standard lamp and depict a cub sitting on father or mother bear's shoulder, supporting the branch which is wired to take two electric light globes. Both bears have glass eyes and are in their original finish, c1912. Courtesy Jenefer Warwick James.

ILLUS. 249. Key wind mechanical Teddies. Both are made in Japan, when wound they walk and drink, c1956. Courtesy Marjory Fainges.

ILLUS.250. A simpler version of the carved wood standard lamp. The bear has glass eyes and is in his original finish, c1912. Courtesy Jenefer Warwick James.

Teddies have been made; these toys were popular in 1930s and 1940s. The Teddy Bear paper doll is now very collectable (see **Paper Dolls**).

Papier-mache confectionery containers in the shape of Teddy Bears were very popular at the beginning of the 1900s.

The Japanese made very colourful jointed Teddy Bears in celluloid during the 1940s and 1950s.

Glass bottles in the shape of Teddy Bears have been made over the years. Avon Teddy Bear perfume bottles were made during the 1970s.

Glass Christmas Tree lights in the shape of Teddy were first produced in Germany, early 1900s, and then after

93

ILLUS. 251. A wind-up mechanical scooter-riding Teddy. 5 3/4in (14cm) tall, glass eyes. When the mechanism is activated the left leg moves around as if propelling the scooter along the ground. Marked on the scooter "Made In U.S. Zone Germany" and "Gebr. M. CMD" Maker unknown c1950. Courtesy Ross Schmidt.

1930 in Japan.

Plastic Teddy Bears made by Kleeware and Rosebud of England were made during the 1950s.

Squeaker toy Teddies were made from vinyl from 1960s (see **Rupert Bear**).

MCZ SCHWEIZER PLUSCHTIERCHEN

(Mutzli)

Made in Switzerland, these quality Teddies can be found containing music boxes (see Musical). Marked with a red and white button in the ear or on the chest inscribed "Swiss Made" "Mutzli MCZ". Usually in the smaller size of 8in (20cm) and 9in (23cm) one type of Mutzli Teddy has rattles in his paws.

Fully jointed, excelsior filled with glass eyes.

MECHANICAL

Mechanical Bears can include the wonderful intricate movements of the Japanese battery-operated mechanical bear to the simple head-moving action of the charming yes-no Teddies.

From the early 1900s firms were including the "new wonder toy", the Teddy Bear, in their clockwork toy lines. In 1909 Sears Roebuck and Company, an American mail-order firm, advertised "Mechanical Tumbling Plush Animals" that were wound by turning the arms. This enabled Teddy (or a plush cat) to turn somersaults when laid on a table.

Mechanical Teddy Bears were usually made by manufacturers of mechanical toys rather than by Teddy Bear manufacturers. The German firms of Bing (see **Bing Gebrüder**) and Schuco (see **Schuco**) are good examples of this. Bing was famous for its clockwork mechanical toys and it would seem only logical that the company would produce me-

ILLUS. 252. Key wind mechanical Teddies. Both made in Japan c1956. Courtesy Marjory Fainges.

chanical Teddy Bears. However some traditional soft Teddies were also produced. Schuco also made the traditional soft-toy Teddy Bears as well as clockwork mechanical versions.

The mechanical Teddies produced by Bing included walking, climbing and tumbling Teddies. The Schuco mechanical Teddy Bears included skating and skiing Teddies as well as the yes-no Teddies.

The French company of Roullet et Decamps (see **Roullet et Decamps**) made clockwork mechanical toys from the late 1800s and these included bears. These wind-up mechanical toys included a drinking and a dancing bear.

Wind-up mechanical bears made of tin are collectable but not as popular as plush fabric covered mechanical Teddy Bears.

MERRYTHOUGHT

The English firm of Merrythought had its beginnings in 1919 as a partnership between W. G. Holmes and G. H. Laxton. At this time Holmes and Laxton opened a small spinning mill in Yorkshire making mohair fabric from imported raw mohair. During the 1920s the partnership suffered a loss of business because of the invention of the cheaper synthetic fibres. As the purchasers of Holmes and Laxton mohair fabric declined, the partnership diversified into soft-toy making, using the mohair fabric

UA54D—English "Merrythought" Teddy Bears. Golden Brown, with growlers. Sizes, prices: 11in., **23/6**; 13in., **35/6**; 16in., **45/6**; 21in., **59/6**.

ILLUS. 253. Advertised Christmas 1955, Courtesy Grace Bros. Sydney.

that they themselves were producing. The company began making toys in 1930 in Coalbrookdale (now Ironbridge) in Shropshire and in 1931 the Merrythought catalogues included Teddy Bears.

The Merrythought Company also produces dolls and Golliwoggs as well as all types of soft toy animals, novelty nightwear cases and push-along and ride-on toys, balls, glove toys, rattles, hobby horses and flexi-toys.

Over the years Merrythought has made many well-known characters including the MGM characters Tom and Jerry, the very collectable Bonzo, Dinkie, Noddy and Big Ears, the Lawson Woods-designed monkeys and the ever-popular Walt Disney characters Snow White and the Seven Dwarves, Mickey Mouse, Donald Duck, Pluto, the characters from "Lady and the Tramp", Thumper Rabbit and the A. A. Milne characters from the Walt Disney production of Winnie the Pooh.

The Merrythought Teddy Bear must be considered amongst the best in the world. The Teddy Bears can be made from several different materials including the traditional mohair plush, long mohair, art silk, woolly plush, modacrylic plush, silk plush, and nylon. Traditional Teddies are fully jointed and kapok filled.

Merrythought Teddies are tagged to the foot with a sewn-on cloth tag and have a cardboard swing tag in the shape of a wishbone (the company's registered trademark).

The woven cloth foot tag on Teddies made before 1939 reads, "Merrythought - Hygienic Toys - Made in England". These early Merrythought Teddies also had a button in their ear (see **Buttons**).

ILLUS. 254. The Merrythought celluloid covered metal button. The button reads, "HYGIENIC MERRYTHOUGHT TOY, MADE IN ENGLAND. Regd Trade Mark."

ILLUS. 255. Merrythought tag from before World War II, "Merrythought Hygienic Toys Made in England".

ILLUS.256. Merrythought tag from after World War II. "Ironbridge, Shropshire, Made in England".

Production of soft toys, including Teddy Bears, was interrupted soon after World War II commenced when the factory then produced goods required for the war effort. When production resumed in 1947, the cloth foot tag was printed and read, "Merrythought Ironbridge, Shropshire Made in England".

This very imaginative firm produces all types of soft-toy animals, dolls, traditional Teddies, dressed and character Teddies (see **Cheeky, Punkinhead, Beefeater**).

MINIATURES

Many German companies have made miniature Teddy Bears over the years. Probably the most popular and well-known were made by the firms of Schuco (see **Schuco**) and Steiff

ILLUS. 258. Two beautiful miniature Teddy Bears. The one on the left is 1 3/4in (4.5cm) tall, unjointed and his clothes are removable. The one on the right is 2in (5cm) tall with a movable head, the body and limbs are moulded in one piece. Courtesy Nancy Finlayson.

(see **Steiff**). Other German manufacturers include Hermann and Clemens.

The Japanese manufactured a miniature bear with an unjointed neck from the 1930s until the early 1960s. These were usually excelsior filled wire-jointed, made from synthetic plush and with glass eyes.

English manufacturers made little Teddies of 8in to 10in (20.3cm - 25.4cm) but did not appear to make any miniatures.

Australian companies also appeared

ILLUS. 257. Three miniature Steiff Teddies. The two Teddies on the left are 6 1/2in (16cm) tall and the Teddy on the right is 5 1/2in (14cm) tall. Courtesy L. Albright.

ILLUS. 261. A beautiful large 28in (71cm) Merrythought Teddy Bear. Tagged to the right foot "Merrythought Hygienic Toy, Made in England" c1946. Fully jointed, quality mohair fabric, kapok filled. Note the distinctive claws, peculiar to some Merrythought Teddy Bears.

ILLUS. 259. An early Merrythought Teddy Bear, 22in (56cm) tall, tagged to the foot "Merrythought-Hygienic Toys, Made in England". Also a button in the ear reads "Hygienic Merrythought Toy, Made in England Regd. Trade Mark". Fully jointed, glass eyes, pale gold mohair

ILLUS. 260. A charming bunny family, made by Merrythought in 1938, known as Bunnihug. Bunnihugs were made in three sizes, 15in (38cm), 18in (46cm) and 21in (53cm). They are unjointed, have glass eyes and the clothes are original. All tagged "Merrythought Hygienic Toys, Made in England". Courtesy Nancye Aitken.

ILLUS. 262. A 12in (30.5cm) Merrythought Teddy Bear. Fully jointed, glass eyes, mohair fabric, kapok filled. The button in his ear has the celluloid covering missing. c1936.

to make their Teddies in the larger sizes, and the same appears true of American-made Teddies.

Miniature Teddy Bears made as Christmas decorations are now available from Taiwan and Hong Kong. These cheap little Teddies are proving very popular.

MISHA

The unjointed Teddy was made and designed by R. Dakin and Company as the official mascot of the 1980 Moscow Olympics. The name was taken from the Russian bear of folklore Mishka (see **Mishka**). Misha wears a belt decorated with the five intertwined Olympic rings. Misha had sold in excess of 75,000 when the Americans boycotted the Olympic games, and so Dakin Americanised the remaining 100,000 bears by stripping off the belt and fitting the bears with multicoloured tee shirts. One featured a hockey player and "USA" another, the slogan "I Am Just A Bear". Dakin also cut the cloth tag to remove any reference to the Olympic Games.

In most cases Mishas on sale in toy shops were stripped of the incriminating five-ring belt and dressed in many different types of clothing. The complete Misha with belt and tag are now collectable.

ILLUS. 263. A wonderful rare hug of miniature Teddies, from left to right. 3 1/2in (9cm) tan Steiff, c1950, 3 1/2in (9cm) tan Steiff c1950, 4in (10cm) pink mohair Teddy early 1900s, (in bath) 3 1/2in (9cm) gold Steiff c1950, 5in (13cm) dark brown Yes-No Schuco. Courtesy L. Albright.

MISHKA

A Russian folklore bear of the 12th Century. A popular bear even today, Mishka was made the subject of a cartoon series in the form of an astronaut emulating the achievements of the Russian spaceman.

The symbol of the 1980 Moscow Olympic Games (see **Misha**).

ILLUS. 265. A 8in (20cm) Misha, tagged on the bottom of the leg "Fun Farm - 1980. San Francisco CA. Product of Korea. All new materials, contents shredded clippings, ground nut shells. 16."

ILLUS. 264. From left to right. A 12in (31cm) Russian made Misha together with a Dakin Misha and a ceramic Misha made in Czechoslovakia. Photograph Courtesy Vera Woodhead.

ILLUS. 266. 1958. Courtesy Australasian Sportsgoods and Toy Retailer.

MORELLA

Mrs Irene Morella was known for many years as "The Koala Bear Lady of Australia". The Morella fur-toy making factory, situated in a suburb of Sydney, NSW, was operated by Mr H. and Mrs. I. Morella from the late 1930s until the death of first Mr Morella and then in 1970 Mrs Morella. The company is still in production today at the same location. The Morella brand fur-toy range include koalas, platypus, kangaroos, pandas and Teddy Bears. A very active lady that worked hard to promote Morella toys and the Australian toy industry in general.

MUSIC BOX

Most Teddy Bears are made with some kind of noisemaker (see **Noise**). The Teddy that contains a music box is very popular in the nursery and has been manufactured by many firms over many years.

There are three different types of music boxes found in Teddy Bears:

1 Wind-up type mechanical;

2 Crank type;

3 Concertina squeeze type;

The wind-up music box Teddy usually has the key to the music box in his back; however, a Schuco music box Teddy Bear has the key in his chest. A Teddy advertised in 1939 boasted that Teddy contained a Swiss music box "with an embedded key that has no sharp edges to cut the child". Many Teddies were advertised to contain a music box and all advertisements do seem to specify that the music boxes are "Swiss Made".

During the 1950s the English firm of Chad Valley produced a key-wind music box bear that played "Teddy Bears Picnic" when wound. The Swiss company Mutzli MCZ (see **MCZ**) produced beautiful music-box Teddies, usually in the smaller sizes of 8in (20cm) and 10in (25cm).

Nursery Teddies are still produced today with wind-up music boxes in

ILLUS. 267. An unmarked Teddy Bear with a music box in his torso. The music box is made up of a metal cage containing metal bells. As the Teddy is shaken the bells hit the cage and produce a melodic sound. Teddy is 20in (51cm) tall, fully jointed, cotton plush with cotton paw pads and inner ears, moulded nose and beautiful glass eyes, c1950.

the torso, "Brahms' Lullaby", "Teddy Bears Picnic" and "Rock-a-bye Baby" are still favourites. Some koalas produced in Australia for the tourist trade contain wind-up music boxes that play "Waltzing Matilda". It would appear that the crank-type music box is not as popular as a wind-up clockwork version, as not as many examples are found. Again the little winder handle was usually placed in the back of the bear.

Probably the most charming of all music-box Teddies is the concertina squeeze-box type. The Teddy must be held around his mid-section with two hands and gently squeezed. Some versions of the concertina music box play a definite tune while others simply produce beautiful melodic notes at random.

This type of Teddy was advertised in the 1929 Sears, Roebuck catalogue for $3.98.

F.A.0. Schwarz's Christmas catalogues of 1932 and 1935 offered a Teddy that played music "with a gentle hug".

Firms that produced musical Teddy Bears include:

Chad Valley
Dean's
Helvetic
Schuco
Steiff

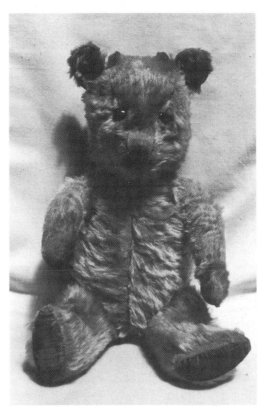

LEFT
ILLUS. 268. This Chiltern Teddy Bear has a squeeze type music box in his torso. A pretty tinkling melody is played when Teddy is squeezed gently. Fully jointed with velvet paw pads and glass eyes c1950s, from the Hugme range of Chiltern Teddies.

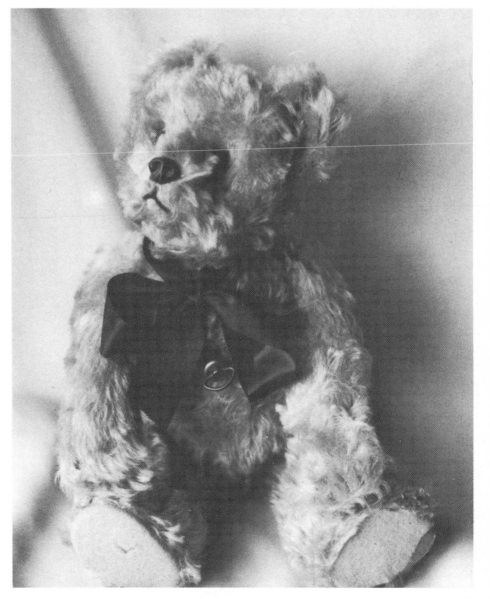

RIGHT.
ILLUS. 269. A rare and beautiful musical Schuco Yes-No Teddy, the winder is in the chest, moulded nose, glass eyes, long mohair fabric. Cardboard inner soles and turned-over paws add to the appeal of this lovely Teddy. It is interesting to note that the original pink colouring has faded to a soft grey. Courtesy Lesley Hurford.

RIGHT
ILLUS. 270. Two rare white Steiff muzzle bears, c1913. The bears are fully jointed, shoe-button eyes, with their original muzzles. Courtesy Sotheby's Auctions, London.

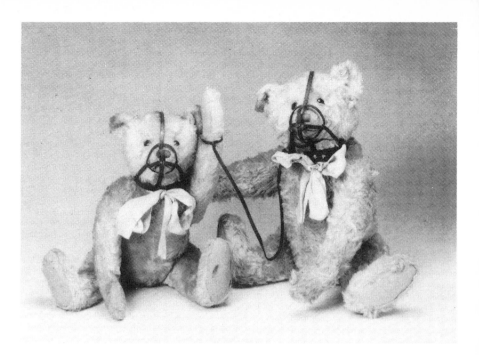

BELOW
ILLUS. 271. A rare Steiff muzzle bear c1913. Cinnamon plush with felt paw pads, fully jointed, shoe-button eyes, original leather muzzle. Courtesy Sotheby's Auctions, London.

MUTZLI
(see **MCZ Schweizer Plüschtier-chen**)

MUZZLE
The snout, the nose and mouth of an animal, or Teddy Bear.
Some Teddy Bears have shaved muzzles, some have their muzzles made from contrasting materials or in contrasting colours.

MUZZLE
A leather cage-like contraption that fits over the mouth and nose of an animal to prevent biting.
Steiff produced a Muzzle Teddy Bear from as early as 1908.
Several versions of muzzled bears standing on all fours and mounted on wheels were made during the first quarter of the century.
As muzzles are removable it is rare to find a vintage Teddy complete with his original muzzle.

N

NISBET
(see **House of Nisbet**)

NO FRILLS BEAR
Manufactured by R. Dakin and Company. An unjointed Teddy 11in (28cm) tall in a sitting position, made from light brown heavy cotton. His face is printed in black and on one foot is printed a price code as seen on supermarket goods. Printed on his chest, "Basic, all purpose, durable No Frills Bear TM. Lost in a Designer World. Plain Wrap product. When you could care less about having the very best".

ILLUS. 272. The No-Frills Bear by Dakin.

X.G.—MODERN STOVE. 2 burner, 9 accessories (whistle kettle). Top plate. 8½ x 4in. 37/11. Post 1/10, 3/-.

X.H.—MUSICAL BOX. Turn handle to make it tinkle. 5in. Metal. 5/11. Post 1/5.

X.J.—HANDBAG. For "Dolly." 2 x 1½in. Leather, plus strap. Press button clip, 2/-. Post 5d.

X.K.—EMBROIDERY. 10 x 12in. Cotton, needles. 5 pieces, plus sewing frame. 8/6. Post 1/5.

X.L.—ROLLI EYES. Coloured plush doll. 16in. Eyes that flirt, plastic face, 44/6. Post 1/10, 3/-.

X.M.—COLOURED BEAR with squeaker. 15in. Coloured plush. Glass eyes. 28/3. Post 1/10, 3/-.

X.N.—TINGLE BEAR. 13in. Coloured. Shake to make it ting-a-ling, 45/-. Post 1/5.

X.O.—GOLLIWOG. Black with coloured plush dressing and plastic face. 15in. 41/-. Post 1/10, 3/-.

X.P.—DOLL'S HOUSE. All metal with plastic furniture and motor car. Pressed and beautifully coloured. Doors, etc., all open. Dismantled in carton. 23 x 9 x 11in., 95/11. Post 4/8, 6/-.

Postage: 1st price N.S.W., 2nd Q. or ▼.

45

ILLUS. 273. A page from the trade journal "Playthings" 1956, shows an advertisement for a Tingle Bear. "Shake to make it ting-a-ling", and for a Teddy with a squeaker.

He wears a cardboard tag around his neck and is also tagged to the leg. A well made Teddy designed to look as if he is made from flour sacks.

Made in Korea for R. Dakin and Company, San Francisco, 1985.

NOISE
Most Teddy Bears are made capable of making some kind of noise.

The noise most readily associated with Teddy is a growl (see **Growler**). Growlers were comparatively expensive to fit into a Teddy torso and the press squeaker (see **Squeaker**) was more popular with cost-conscious manufacturers. It is not uncommon to find a veteran Teddy with a bald spot or even a hole worn on his tummy, by overly enthusiastic little owners squeaking the life out of him.

Musical Teddies (see **Music Box**) are very popular with children without being a plus to collectors.

ILLUS. 274. A rare Steiff Rattle Teddy Bear, 5in (13cm) tall, jointed limbs, glass eyes, excelsior filled. Teddy rattles when shaken. c1920s. Courtesy Angela Donovan.

Rattle Teddies were made by several companies, including the English firm of Chiltern (see **Chiltern**).
A Mutzli Teddy (see **MCZ**) has rattles in his paws.
The ting-a-ling type rattle Teddy has a metal cage, holding a small metal ball in the torso producing a delightful musical sound when Teddy is shaken. Steiff (see **Steiff**) produced a version of this type of bear.
Cheeky (see **Cheeky**) by Merrythought has a bell in each ear.
A Teddy advertised in 1925 was described as a "Squawking Teddy Bear".
Burbank Toys produce a pull-string talking Rupert (see **Rupert Bear**) bear, he speaks different sentences when activated. Steiff also make a pull-string "talking" Teddy.

NOSES

Teddy nose styles are many and varied. The most common type of nose is stitched on to the face. However noses can be made from leather, rubber, metal, cloth and plastic. A rare early Steiff Teddy features a nose made from sealing wax.

Stitched noses can be vertical or horizontal with companies using either method so that the method of stitching noses cannot be used as a reliable identification guide. Stitched noses can also be readily replaced, again making identification from nose shape almost impossible. However, Joy Toys (see **Joy Toys**) Teddies do have very distinctively stitched noses with larger outside stitches on a vertically sewn nose. Most stitched noses are black. However Alpha Farnell (see **Farnell, Alpha**) have a style of Teddy with fawn coloured stitched noses, Steiff (see **Steiff**) also made Teddies with fawn stitched noses.
"Jackie" the Jubilee Bear (see **Jackie**) has a distinctive white horizontal stitch on his black vertical stitched nose.

NOVELTY

Novelty describes a Teddy Bear that is something more than a soft toy but has no mechanical or moving parts.
The novelty bears of the German firm Schuco (see **Schuco**) included the compact and perfume bottle Teddies and the two-faced Janus Teddy.
Merrythought also made a novelty two-faced Teddy, one face a traditional Teddy Bear while the other is an orang-outang.

Easy to make.
BEAR'S HEAD.

Everything supplied. Stuffing, glass eyes, all parts complete instructions.

Prepared by War Disabled Men

Toycraft. 19, Roundhay Rd. **Leeds 7. England**

Proprietor - G. Russell Inman.

ILLUS. 275. A novelty bear's head kit, c1916. Offered for sale at a Doll and Teddy Bear Fair in the North of England. Courtesy Jack Tempest.

ILLUS. 276. A Schuco two-faced Teddy Bear known as Janus. 3 1/2in (9cm) tall brown plush mohair fabric, fully jointed. The Teddy Bear face has metal pin eyes and a black embroidered nose and mouth. The novelty face has metal pin eyes and nose, the eyes are backed with white discs. The head is turned by means of a metal knob between the legs. This little bear appears to have lost his mouth. Courtesy Sotheby's Auctions, London .

Other types of novelty Teddy Bears include candy containers, a stand-up hollow torso bear with a removable head, and a bottle container, a conventional head and front limbs attached to a zippered cloth container.
Included in this group is the Teddy Bear muff, tea cosy, pyjama case and purse.
Made by many companies, most of these novelty Teddies are unmarked. However as they were made as gift items and not toys they are usually of a very high quality.
The muff, tea cosy and pyjama case

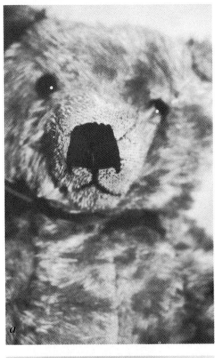

ILLUS. 277. Noses.
  (a) 1940 Merrythought Teddy's nose.
  (b) 1940 Chinese Teddy's nose of moulded rubber.
  (c) 1950 English Teddy's nose of a crudely cut piece of felt stuck on to the muzzle.
  (d) 1960 Alpha Farnell Teddy's blonde nose.
  (e) 1930s unusual nose is a piece of leather sewn on to the muzzle with two stitches. Origin of this bear is unknown.   Excelsior filled, brushed cotton fabric.
  (f) 1940 Well made hand-stitched nose of a Berlex Teddy.
  (g) 1915 Steiff Teddy. The stitching of the nose has worn away leaving the black felt lining showing.

and purse are usually made with a traditional Teddy head.

Not as popular with arctophiles as the Teddy Bear, nevertheless these novelties do add charm and interest to a collection.

103

ILLUS. 278 A Schuco two-faced Teddy Bear known as Janus. 3 1/2in (9cm) tall, fully jointed, gold mohair fabric. The plain Teddy Bear face has metal pin eyes and black embroidered nose and mouth. The novelty face has white discs behind the metal pin eyes, the nose is also a metal pin. The tongue is protruding from the mouth that has white lips. The head is turned by means of a metal knob between the legs. No marks. c1940. Courtesy Jenefer Warwick James.

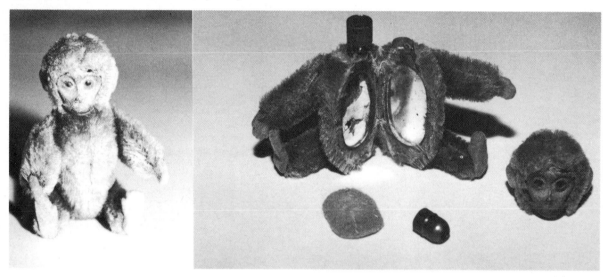

ILLUS. 279. A novelty Schuco compact monkey, 3 1/2in (9cm) tall, jointed limbs, mohair covered tin torso, felt paws, metal flocked face. The head comes off to reveal a lipstick, the torso can then be opened to reveal compact. Made before 1950. Courtesy Angela Donovan.

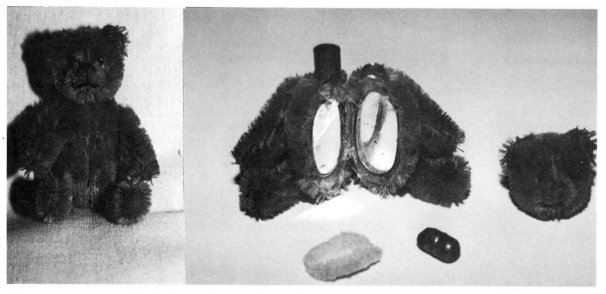

ILLUS. 280. A novelty compact Teddy Bear by Schuco. 3 1/2in (9cm) tall. The head comes off, revealing a lipstick. The torso can then be opened to reveal a powder compact comprising a mirror, a compartment to hold compressed face powder and a tiny powder puff. This photograph shows the torso open, note the powder puff and lipstick in the foreground. Jointed limbs, mohair covered tin torso. Made after 1950. Mint condition. Courtesy Angela Donovan.

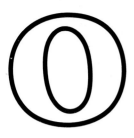

OPEN MOUTH
(see **Laughing Teddy Bears**)
(see **Feed Me Bears**)

OPHELIA
The delightful lady Teddy Bear character pictured in Michele Durkson Clise's book "Ophelia's World". The Steiff interpretation of this Teddy Bear of the same name is white, wearing a lacy collar, fully jointed, standing 16 1/2in (42cm) tall, with a growler.

ILLUS. 282. Ophelia's World by Michele Durkson Clise.

ILLUS. 281. A rare open-mouth bear on wheels. Mohair fabric, glass eyes, two claws on each foot, excelsior filled. The bear is unmarked but the wheels are marked FLORESTA. (See **German Teddy Bears-Scheyer and Co.**) c1930. Courtesy Obie Bronte.

ILLUS. 283. The Steiff Ophelia Bear, 16 1/2in (42cm) tall. Made of white mohair, fully jointed, wearing a versatile, ruffled collar of point d'esprit. Ophelia comes complete in her own lace patterned presentation box. Courtesy Steiff.

Lettie Lane Introduces Betty Bonnet's Little Sister and Her Nurse

By Sheila Young

ILLUS. 284. A beautiful big Teddy is featured in this Ladies Home Journal Lettie Lane series, c1916. Entitled Lettie Lane Introduces Betty Bonnet's Little Sister and Her Nurse, by Sheila Young.

P Q

PADDINGTON

Paddington Bear is the brainchild of writer Michael Bond who bought a lonely little Teddy from Selfridge's department store in London as a last-minute Christmas gift for his wife in 1956. Michael Bond created the adventures of a Teddy Bear found in Paddington railway station (hence his

ILLUS. 285. The 19in (48cm) tall English-made Paddington Bear by Gabrielle Designs. A much heavier, more solid bear than the Eden Paddington, unjointed with a moulded plastic nose. This Paddington wears his original wool felt duffle coat and Dunlop rubber boots. Tagged to the back centre seam with a white satin tag printed in blue "Hand made in England by Gabrielle Designs. U.K. Reg. Design No 957892" together with design numbers for Australia, Canada, New Zealand, South Africa. "This bear ©1972 Gabrielle Designs Ltd."

name) after a journey from Peru. He was wearing a label stating, "Please look after this bear. Thank you". The original Paddington books by Michael Bond are illustrated by Peggy Fortrum. Mr Bond describes Paddington as "not a cuddly bear - he's a bear for standing in corners,

that's why he wears Wellington boots". Paddington is fond of wearing a duffle coat and eating marmalade.

Paddington appears on television in many countries, is the subject of eleven books and models of Paddington sell more than a hundred thousand yearly. The original Paddington was made in England, tagged to the back centre seam, "Hand Made in England by Gabrielle Designs" with registered design numbers for UK, Australia, New Zealand, Canada, South Africa, 18in (45.7cm) tall, unjointed, plastic eyes and moulded black plastic nose. He wears Dunlop rubber boots, wool felt duffle coat and a felt sou-wester rain hat with the front brim pinned back with a safety pin. Hanging from his coat is his famous luggage tag, "Darkest Peru to London, England, via Paddington Station" on one side and "Please look after this bear, thank you" on the other.

ILLUS. 286. Two miniature Paddington Bears 1 1/2in (3.5cm) tall, Paddington on the left is made of pottery, while Paddington on the right is flock-covered plastic. The hat and the baggage tag are removable. Courtesy Nancy Finlayson.

The American company Eden, manufactures Paddington in many sizes with an unjointed body, plastic eyes and a sewn nose. The duffle coat is brushed cotton and because of Ameri-

ILLUS. 287. These soft filled Paddingtons are made by Eden Toys Inc. Both are all original, and both are unjointed. Tagged to the left leg with a white woven tag with blue writing "Copyright © Eden Toys, Inc. 1975, 1981 New York, N.Y., U.S.A. Produced in Korea under licence of Paddington and Co Ltd, London, England". The Paddington in the P.B. sweater is 13in (33cm) tall, the Paddington in the chef's hat is 8in (20cm) tall. Courtesy Debra Aldridge.

can safety laws, the sou-wester does not carry a safety pin. The Wellington boots are marked on the sole "P B" in reverse together with the Eden copyright. Tagged to the leg "Copyright Eden Toys, Inc. 1975, 1981, New York, NY, USA. Produced in Korea under license of Paddington and Co Ltd, London, England".

A tiny plaster figure is available in England as a tourist souvenir. Simplicity Patterns offers a pattern for a Paddington Bear to be made at home. Even without the tags it is easy to tell the difference between a Paddington made by Gabrielle Designs and Eden Toys Inc. The English Gabrielle is much firmer filled and quite heavy. The fabric is a cotton plush. The Eden Paddington is soft filled, very light, and the fabric is a synthetic plush. Paddington is reputed to be the highest money earner in the Teddy Bear world.

PANDAS

The Teddy Bear's cousin, the black and white panda has never enjoyed the popularity of Teddy and not as many panda bears have been produced. However most Teddy Bear manufacturers include a panda in their range of bears.

Almost every company produces a different combination of the black and white panda coat. However all pandas do have black patches on their eyes and the torso is usually white.

Pandas can be found jointed the same as a traditional Teddy Bear or unjointed standing on all fours.

PAPER DOLLS

From the early 1900s Cut-out Teddy Bear Paper Dolls were produced.

ILLUS. 288. Two 7in (18cm) tall paper Teddy Bears, one with a clown costume and the other with a sailor costume by McLoughlin Bros, U.S.A. Courtesy Marvin Cohen Auctions.

They were offered as give-aways by publishing and manufacturing companies. The Boston Sunday Globe in USA printed a series of cut-out Teddies with different costumes in each weekly publication during 1907-1908. These included Teddy Bear with a Dutchman's suit, an Indian suit, a sailor suit etc.

The American toy trade magazine "Playthings" reported in 1907 that "The Teddy Bear Paper Doll, as it is called, is a very fascinating toy, and no child whether girl or boy would want to be without one. The new toy can be purchased at retail for ten cents, and will afford the youngster a great deal of amusement".

Over the years many sets of cut-out Teddy Bear Paper Dolls were pro-

ILLUS. 289 Pieces cut from an Australian publication c1909. 4 1/4in (11cm) tall.

duced in several countries. Cut-out paper dolls were often depicted holding a Teddy Bear and collectors of paper Teddies can often find lovely examples of paper Teddies in these sets. The "Lettie Lane" series of paper dolls published in the American "The Ladies' Home Journal" is an example of this.

Probably the most well-known and collectable is the "Teddy Bear Paper Doll" set published by J. Ottoman Lithographing Co, New York, in the early 1900s. This set comprises an envelope holding a set of pre-cut Teddy clothes on paper and a Teddy printed on heavy cardboard with fixed tags enabling him to stand. This set has recently been reproduced for today's market.

PARKER

An Australian company producing soft toys during the 1960s and 1970s. Several different styles of Teddy Bears were produced as well as pandas and other soft-toy animals.

PAWS AND PAW PADS

Paws are the end of Teddy Bear's limbs. Most Teddies have paw pads; however, as a cost-cutting measure some Teddies do not have paw pads. Most miniature Teddies do not have paw pads. Paw pads are made from:

ILLUS. 290. A beautiful quality English panda. Fully jointed, glass eyes, long mohair fabric, velvet paw pads, wrap around black claws, kapok filled. c1940.

ILLUS. 293. An early Lindee panda c1945, fully jointed, glass eyes, oil cloth paw pads. Courtesy Marjory Fainges.

ILLUS. 295. An Emil panda, jointed limbs, glass eyes, tagged in the centre back seam, "Emil Toys Made in Australia". c1970.

ILLUS. 291. An Alpha Farnell panda 5in (13cm) tall, jointed limbs, one glass eye. Tagged on the left leg with a label "Farnell Alpha Toys. Made in England" c1930.

RIGHT
ILLUS. 292. A 12in (31cm) unjointed panda. Synthetic plush, tagged to the right side seam, "Farnell, Alpha Hygienic Soft Toy Made in England". Courtesy Ross Schmidt.

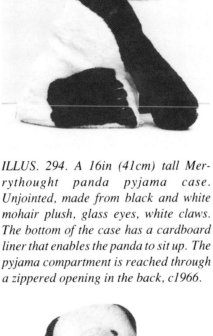

ILLUS. 294. A 16in (41cm) tall Merrythought panda pyjama case. Unjointed, made from black and white mohair plush, glass eyes, white claws. The bottom of the case has a cardboard liner that enables the panda to sit up. The pyjama compartment is reached through a zippered opening in the back, c1966.

ILLUS. 296. An English panda c1940. Fully jointed, glass eyes, velvet paw pads with black wrap-around claws. The ears on this panda are cut into the head.

ILLUS. 297. Two rare Steiff pandas. The larger one is c1940, 8 1/2in (21cm) tall, fully jointed, glass eyes, open mouth, turned down paws. The smaller panda is 6in (15cm) tall c1950. Courtesy L. Albright.

109

ILLUS. 298. A Papa Bear and Baby Bear paper doll set. The Teddies are printed on stiff cardboard while the clothes are printed on paper. Unmarked, papa is 8in (20cm) tall and baby is 6in (15cm), probably English c1940.

ILLUS. 299. Pieces from a rare Rupert Bear paper doll set, c1940. Courtesy Daily Express Newspaper, U.K.

rattles (see **MCZ**). Rear paws pads can have maker's tags sewn onto them.

Steiff's Dicky Bear has his paw pads painted with the details of toes and claws.

After a hard-working life of devotion, veteran Teddies can have replaced paw pads in many and varied materials depending on what is available at the time of surgery. Arctophiles don't mind.

PEDIGREE

The English firm of Pedigree was founded some time before 1938 in London as doll and soft-toy manufacturers.

In 1968 Pedigree was taken over by a Lines Bros company, Rovex Industries Pty Ltd. After the collapse of the Lines Bros company in 1972, Pedigree was taken over by Dumbee Combex Marse Company and finally in 1980 by Tamwade Ltd.

During their years of production, Pedigree factories were situated in the U.K., South Africa, Northern Ireland, New Zealand and Australia.

This imaginative English firm produced quality Teddy Bears and soft toys in many designs including traditional Teddy Bears. The Teddy Bears were available with growlers, squeakers or music boxes. A "cuddle toy" unjointed Teddy was also produced in a nursery line and pram toy line.

Brushed cotton
Felt
Leather
Leatherette
Oilcloth
Rexine
Velvet
Vinyl

Several versions of Teddy Bears have distinguishing paw pads. The Zotty (see **Zotty**) Teddy has turned down front paws. Most Australian Teddies (see **Australian Teddy Bears**) have pointed upturned front paws. Teddy Baby by Steiff (see **Teddy Baby**) has cardboard lining innersoles in his rear paws to enable him to stand unaided. Other unmarked Teddy Bears also have this type of paw. Paws can hide

ILLUS. 300. The Parker Toys' stand at the 1971 Toys and Games Manufacturer's Association Show in Sydney, Australia. There are approximately ten different types of Teddy Bears on display. Courtesy Australasian Sportsgoods and Toy Retailer.

PARKER TOYS for Playmates

NEW FOR '72

59 22" CLOWN

68 13" PLUSH BEAR (Washable)

34 36" PLUSH PANDA (Washable)

See the full Parker selection plus our new range of JULIE BARRY SOFT TOYS at the

TAGMA TOY SHOW

Southern Cross Hotel, Melbourne
JULY 16 to 18

PARKER TOYS PTY. LTD.
131 Johnston St. Fitzroy Vic 3065
Phone - 419 1777

45 PLUSH NURSERY SACHET (Washable)

54 HAPPY FRED 16"-BEAR (Washable)

ILLUS. 301. Advertisement for Parker Toys in June 1972. Courtesy Australasian Sportsgoods and Toy Retailer.

Several "chassis toys" were produced, including pull-along and push-along dogs, horses and donkeys, but it would appear no bears. The jointed Teddies produced during 1930s, 1940s and 1950s could be tagged on the back in the centre seam, fitted with glass eyes and filled with kapok.

LEFT
ILLUS. 301.a. A beautiful Pedigree Teddy Bear 23in (58cm) tall, fully jointed, long mohair fabric, velvet paw pads, glass eyes, tip-up growler in the torso. Tagged in the back centre seam "Pedigree - Made in England". c1950.

LEFT AND BELOW
ILLUS. 302. The cover and two pages of a 1950s Pedigree catalogue. Courtesy Marjory Fainges.

ABOVE
ILLUS. 303. **Is it bed time?** These two old friends are an Alpha Farnell novelty pyjama-case dog and a Steiff Teddy Bear. They are curled up on an early American quilt c1920. The dog has excelsior filled legs and head, glass eyes, and is made of long mohair. He has a quilted satin compartment in his torso to hide pyjamas. Teddy is blonde mohair, fully jointed, excelsior filled, shoe-button eyes and light coloured embroidered nose and mouth. His paw pads are replaced. He is admiring his antique gold pocket watch -he holds it because he doesn't have a pocket! Courtesy Ruth Floth.

LEFT
ILLUS. 304. **All dressed up.** Four little Schuco bears talk hats and parasols and secrets. Their secret is they are compact bears, except the little Teddy on the extreme right. She hides a perfume bottle. Courtesy Angela Donovan.

PERFUME BOTTLE
(see **Novelty**)
(see **Schuco**)

PETER BEAR

A rare and wonderful laughing Teddy Bear (see **Laughing Teddies**). These 14in (35.5cm) Teddies were found mint and in boxes in a toy shop in Germany in 1976 and brought to the UK and USA, and so all Peter Bears found on today's market are usually in mint condition complete with cardboard tags and usually with their box! The bears were made in Germany in 1925 by the Gebrüder Süssenguth factory in Neustadt in Thuringia. Fully jointed and made from the finest mohair, the Teddies are usually of variegated colours of brown and beige; a gold-coloured "Peter" was also made. Excelsior filled.

Peter Bear has large googly eyes that move from side to side when the head is turned. Most of these Teddies were made with wooden eyes; however, some were made with glass. The open mouth of Peter Bear has two rows of carved white teeth and a tongue. The tongue moves from side to side when the head is moved.

The original chest tag reads, "Peter Ges Gesch Nr 895257", while on the original box the label shows a picture of Peter and the slogan, "Neuheit Bar Wie Lebend" ("Novelty. Bear - most natural finish).

ILLUS. 306. A Peter Bear, in his original box showing his chest tag "Peter Ges Gesch Nr 895257". Courtesy Sotheby's Auctions London.

ILLUS. 305. The 1987 Steiff Petsy Teddy. Fully jointed, the fabric is surface washable. Courtesy Steiff.

PETSY

A popular Steiff Teddy Bear first issued in 1928. The Petsy style of Teddy Bear was first named Buschy and then underwent a name change to Petsy. The early Petsy is 14in (36cm) tall, soft filled, fully jointed made in long-haired brown mohair with white tips. The ears of Petsy are filled with wires enabling them to be posed into different positions. Two versions of Petsy were made, one with a red nose and claws and blue eyes, and one with brown nose and claws and brown eyes.

A Steiff Teddy Bear reported to be a Petsy created a world record price when sold at auction by Sotheby's London in September 1989, for 55,000 pounds sterling. Steiff later described the record breaking Teddy to be a "one off" and not a Petsy.

Petsy was re-released in the 1960s as a soft filled, fully jointed Teddy made from dralon. The popular Petsy is still made in the 1980s.

PETZ

A German Teddy Bear manufactured from 1948 to the 1960s. A fully jointed, excelsior filled Teddy with glass eyes. The Petz Teddy can have a cloth tag or a glass button or both. The tag reads "Original Petz US Zone", the button has "Petz" printed on it.

PHOTOGRAPHS

In the days before the cost of a camera was within the reach of most families, a studio portrait photograph was taken at important moments in life, such as weddings, christenings and birthdays.

A child having perhaps a birthday photograph taken would be stood beside a piece of furniture (to hang on to) and given a toy to hold to soothe the nerves. What better than the company of a Teddy Bear to help get through the ordeal? Now sought after by collectors of old photographs as well as Teddy collectors, the studio photo of a child and a Teddy Bear is a treasure.

PICCOLO
(see **Schuco**)

ILLUS. 308. Love is a big sister and an old panda bear, c1960. Photograph courtesy Bradley Forgeard.

ILLUS. 307. A 24in (61cm) Steiff Petsy Teddy. Blue and black eyes, brown embroidered nose and mouth, fully jointed, light coloured mohair with darker tip, c1927. Courtesy Sotheby's Auctions, London.

ILLUS. 309. This family photo is very early, c1905. Note Teddy has external jointing. The photographer's premises were in View Street, Bendigo, Australia.

ILLUS. 310. A rare Schuco Panda perfume bottle, with jointed limbs. The head conceals the neck of a perfume bottle. Pin-head eyes, black embroidered nose and mouth c1950. Courtesy Angela Donovan.

ILLUS. 311. "The Game of Teddy Bear" c1907. The original Teddy Bear game of cards. Made by the Teddy Bear Novelty Company, Silver Springs, N.Y. Courtesy David Worland.

LEFT
ILLUS. 312. This English set of playing cards comprises ten sets of four cards of Mother, Father, Miss and Master Bear participating in some activity, c1940. Maker unknown.

ABOVE
ILLUS. 313. A set of three of the "Merry Message" series printed in England. Each card is embossed in gold "At Woy Woy, N.S.W." c 1950.

ILLUS. 314. "One of us must die" copyright 1908, Campbell Art Co, N.Y. Posted in London on December 23rd, 1909.

RIGHT
ILLUS. 315. "Breakfast in bed". One of the "Oilette" series of humorous postcards published by Raphael Tuck and Sons, of England.

117

ILLUS. 316. Courtesy of the N.S.W. State Library.

ILLUS. 318. Ashley John Skinner, aged one year in 1970, enjoying the company of his Lindee Teddy. He still enjoys Ted's company in 1990.

ILLUS. 317. Baby Helen Wiegard with her lambswool panda "Pamela Grace" won in Melbourne in 1948. Photo courtesy Faye Wiegard.

ABOVE
ILLUS. 319. Taken in November 1926, a photograph of the Queen Mother, then Duchess of York, with a Dean's Teddy Bear presented to her by the school children of Ilford, England. Photograph courtesy David Worland.

ABOVE RIGHT
ILLUS. 320. This photographic postcard is marked "Rotary Photo, London. E. C. Printed in England".

RIGHT
ILLUS. 321. This photographic postcard was taken in 1910. The subject is baby Gerry Worland, father of well known arctophile David Worland. Courtesy David Worland.

LEFT
ILLUS. 322. A beautiful 26in (68cm) fully marked PETZ Teddy Bear. Fully jointed, excelsior filled, glass eyes, gold mohair, pink felt paw pads. The ears are cut into the head. This important Teddy still retains his glass PETZ button on his chest and his white rayon tag woven in blue with the words " Original PETZ US Zone Germany." Teddy was made after 1946 but still has an "early" look about him. His nose and claws are embroidered in black and Teddy still has a very active growler in his torso.

RIGHT
ILLUS. 323. A rare Campaign Teddy Bear by Ideal. These 12in (31cm) Teddies were given away during the 1905 campaign to re-elect President Roosevelt. Teddy wears a President Roosevelt gold framed brooch. Courtesy David Worland.

LEFT
ILLUS. 324. A rare 1904 Roosevelt campaign item. A pressed glass plate featuring Teddies at play. Courtesy David Worland.

BELOW
ILLUS. 325. "The Roosevelt Bears, Their Travels and Adventures" by Seymour Eaton. This is the first book in the series and page 11 shows Teddy B and Teddy G ready to go on their travels. This picture from page 165 is the well dressed and sophisticated Teddy B and Teddy G "doing Fifth Avenue".

PLAYING CARDS

As with all children's games, playing cards have also been decorated with Teddy Bears, and manufactured since the early 1900s by many different companies from many countries. "The Three Bears" was produced as a card game by Milton Bradley Co USA 1920.

"Playthings", the toy trade magazine of the USA, states in 1907 "the recent release of a parlour game is the Teddy Bear Card Game which retails for 50c, the pack consists of 132 cards and three different games can be played."

ILLUS. 326. A miniature set of Teddy decorated playing cards 1 3/4in (4.5cm) x 1 1/4in (3cm) c1950. Maker unknown.

POLAR BEARS

The soft toy Polar Bear is usually made of white fabric and standing on all four feet. It is rare to find a jointed Polar Bear. The Polar Bear is usually made with a longer neck and smaller head than cousin Teddy.

Most soft toy-making companies offer a Polar Bear in their range but this white cousin of the Teddy Bear is by no means as popular as Teddy. Steiff has produced many Polar Bears throughout the years, including a life-size 62in (157.4 cm) version with a swivel head sitting upright on his back legs. Another version is fully jointed. The English firm of Dean's produced Polar Bears during the

122

ILLUS. 327. A rare white leather polar bear. 5in (13cm) tall, 10in (25cm) long. The nose is moulded plastic, the eyes glass, the mouth is lined in red leather, c1948.

1930s, these in several sizes. The Dean's Polar Bear has a leather nose, glass eyes, and is unjointed.

The French firm of Roullet et Decamps (see **Roullet et Decamps**) produced a wind-up mechanical Polar Bear standing upright on a papier mache rock. The bear opens and closes his mouth and nods his head. Merrythought produced a Polar Bear standing on all fours, 1957. This white silk plush bear has bells in his ears.

POLISH

Teddy Bears manufactured in Poland were exported to many countries during the 1950s to 1970s. The Teddies were unmarked or marked with the name of the distributor.

Usually made of a lesser quality plush fabric, often cotton plush, firmly filled with excelsior, glass eyes and fully jointed.

Shackman and Co, released a Teddy School boxed set in 1970 containing six miniature Polish Teddy Bear pupils. These are unjointed with bendable wire limbs. They each bear an oval paper tag "Made in Poland".

POOH BEAR
(see **Winnie the Pooh**)

ILLUS. 328. An advertisement for Polish toys including Teddy Bears, August 1965. Courtesy Australasian Sportsgoods and Toy Retailer.

POSTCARDS

The postcard has been a popular form of communication since the late 1890s. Since the 1930s the use of the postcard declined to such a degree that it was almost exclusively used as a carrier of a message from someone on holidays. That can still be said today. However during the first two decades of this century the postcard was a reliable, cheap and quick method of communicating, and was almost indispensable in the everyday life of the Edwardian household. Christmas, New Year and birthday greetings were carried on the humble postcard, but so were the everyday messages. Appointments were made by tradespeople and ladies and gentlemen who intended to call for tea. Collecting postcards became a popular pastime.

The popularity of Teddy made him an ideal subject for the postcard. Teddy could be found drawn or photographed either with or without children in contrived situations.

Many famous illustrators drew Teddies to be printed on postcards. Sometimes a series was produced. Mabel Lucy Attwell often included a Teddy in her illustrations. The Lawson Woods' illustrations of Teddies are very popular. The Roosevelt Bears were featured on a series of postcards published by Edward Stern and Co of USA. These illustrations were lifted from the Roosevelt Bear books by Seymour Eaton.

The quality of the postcard can vary from publisher to publisher. Raphael Tuck and Sons and Valentine's produced beautiful quality colourful postcards. However, a very large percentage of postcards are unmarked.

Teddy Bear postcards are very popular with both the Teddy Bear collector and the postcard collector.

PRE-TEDDY

A term used to describe toy bears made before 1903. Many toy makers made toy bears including Roullet et Decamps (see **Roullet et Decamps**). Steiff produced a bear Roly-Poly toy in 1897.

ILLUS. 329. "Teddy's Chums" Published in London, printed in Saxony.

ILLUS. 330. "Taking the Count" Printed in Germany. Posted in London, c1912.

ILLUS. 331. Printed by H.V. and Co. Ltd., London, this postcard is postmarked London, 1910.

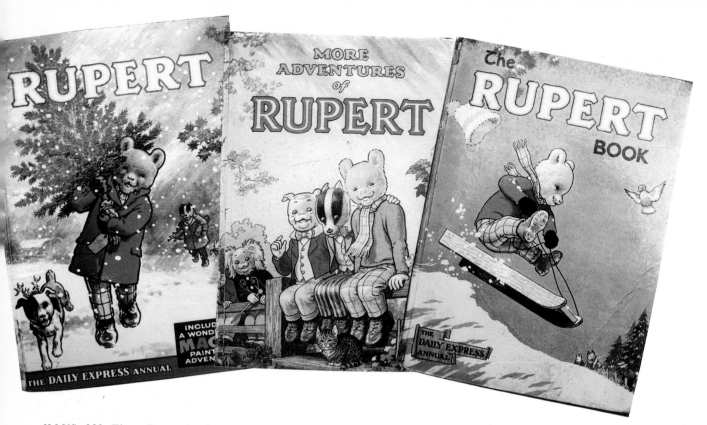

ILLUS. 332. Three Rupert books, "The Daily Express Annual" from the 1960s, drawn by Alfred Bestall. Reproduced by kind permission of the Express Newspapers plc.

ILLUS. 333. An 18in (46cm) tall, Schuco Teddy Bear. Fully jointed, gold mohair fabric, excelsior filled, shaved muzzle, clear glass eyes, black embroidered nose and claws. The feet have cardboard inner soles. A very personable Teddy c1930s.
RIGHT
ILLUS. 334. A very elegant, 16in (41cm) Schuco Teddy, all dressed for an important evening in his top hat, bow tie and cane c1940s. Fully jointed, excelsior filled, glass eyes, long mohair fabric with short mohair muzzle and feet. The feet have cardboard soles. These chubby Teddies are very popular with collectors. This one has a music box in his torso as an added extra. Courtesy Dot Gillett.

ILLUS. 335. A rare dark brown coloured Steiff Teddy Bear, fully jointed, glass eyes, long mohair fabric, felt paw pads, black embroidered nose, mouth and claws. A button in his ear. c1910. Courtesy Debra Aldridge.

ILLUS. 336. A beautiful 16in (41cm) Steiff 1904 Teddy Bear. Fully jointed, shoe-button eyes, black nose, mouth and claws, excelsior filled, pronounced hump and long arms and feet. Button in the ear. Courtesy Helen Jones.

ILLUS. 337. Three new Steiff Teddy Bears. Left, the Richard Steiff Teddy, centre the Original Teddy and the Jackie Teddy replica. The Richard Steiff Teddy and the Jackie Teddy are from the "collector" series and carry a white tag, the Original Teddy is sold as a toy and carries a yellow tag.

ILLUS. 338. Two in a series of photographic postcards with a Christmas message. Marked "Printed in Germany".

ILLUS. 339. Two postcards of photographs of dressed Teddy Bears. These cards feature glass side-glancing googly eyes. Marked only H/B.

ILLUS. 340. "The Old Christmas Wish" Published by E. A. Schwerdtleger and Co. London, E.C., printed at their works in Berlin.

ILLUS. 341. "I Can't bear to be parted from you" by artist Lawson Woods. A Valentine's postcard, printed in Great Britain.

ILLUS. 342. This photograph is marked on the back "Kodak - Austral" "Grace Bros. - Sydney" c1910. The toddler is holding Teddy's ear, instead of his arm.

ILLUS. 343. An unmarked and unused postcard.

ILLUS. 344. A black and white photographic postcard, unmarked, beside undecipherable scrolled initials in the left corner.

ILLUS. 345. A rare Raphael Tuck and Sons postcard. A tear-off card designed to be coloured. Posted July, 1908.

127

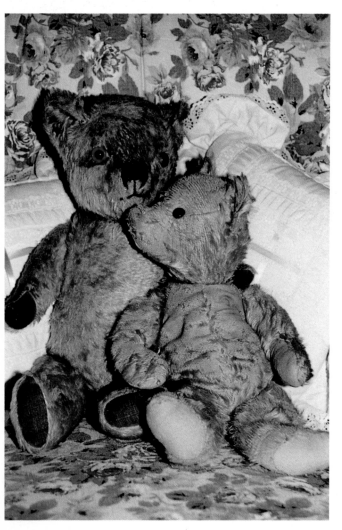

RIGHT
ILLUS. 346. These two vintage toys were owned
by Australian actress Thea Rowe M.B.E. They
were purchased in Perth, Australia, in 1919. In the
early 1920s, Thea Rowe played the part on stage of
Christopher Robin in an A. A. Milne, Winnie the
Pooh play. Ms Rowe recalled that the furniture
had been made on a very large scale so that she had
looked very small. This wonderful old Teddy
played the part of Winnie the Pooh. This "cele-
bearty" is 24in (61cm) tall, fully jointed, excelsior
filled, the ears are cut into the head, the mohair
fabric very bristly, felt paw pads, black embroidered nose, mouth and claws. No markings. The
lithographed doll is named Gracie. She is 24in
(61cm) tall, soft filled, and her underwear is
printed on. She wears her contemporary clothes
that hide many mends. Unmarked. Australian
made.

LEFT
ILLUS. 347. Even though these two Teddies are a
generation apart, they spent several years together
hiding in the bottom of a wardrobe in the home of
a policeman in a Sydney suburb. The policeman's
Teddy was up for sale, when he remembered that
his wife's mother had given her old bear to his
children (her grandchildren) to play with. Out of
the bottom of the wardrobe they came where they
had lain, comforting one another, waiting to be
remembered. They now share an important place
on a shelf in a large hug. The Teddy on the right is
a 17in (43cm) tall Alpha Farnell, fully jointed,
kapok filled, original glass eyes, nose, mouth and
claws embroidered in fawn. He has replaced paw
pads and a very bald torso. Bought in 1929 in
Edinburgh, Scotland. The Teddy on the left is 20in
(51cm) tall, fully jointed, unmarked but made in
England. Kapok filled, the muzzle is excelsior
filled. He has beautiful big glass eyes, quality mohair fabric in excellent condition, velvet paw pads.
The very distinctive nose and mouth are embroidered in black, he has no claws. Bought in Sydney,
Australia, in 1949.

PROVENANCE

To a collector of Teddy Bears probably the most exciting thing about collecting (after finding a wonderful Teddy) is to find an old Teddy with provenance: to know exactly how old Teddy is, who he was bought for, where he was bought from, how much he cost originally, and how he has ended up in one's possession.

In an extensive collection perhaps only three or four Teddies will have their provenance as the Teddies have probably come through the hands of dealers or from auctions. The dealer will have bought Teddy from garage sales, trash and treasure markets, "door knocks" or house clearance sales and Teddy's secret past remains just that - a secret. My experience is that if a dealer does know the provenance of an old Teddy, he is usually only too pleased to be able to pass it on with the bear.

Auction houses have the confidentiality of their clients to protect but in some cases may be able to supply some provenance on a particular bear purchase.

If one is fortunate enough to acquire the provenance of a Teddy, do write it down immediately. Facts, names and dates can be forgotten in the excitement of a purchase. The written information should then be attached in some way to the bear, not easy if Teddy is not dressed. However I have found that a small piece of paper containing all the pertinent details can be pinned to Teddy's ribbon and folded inside the folds out of sight.

It is essential that any history of an old Teddy remains with him. These facts can then be passed on and perhaps help to unravel the mystery surrounding the origins of so many old Teddies.

We collectors are only stewards of our Teddy collection. We do have a duty to pass on any provenance.

PUNKINHEAD

Made by Merrythought of England (see **Merrythought**) especially for Eaton's Department Store in Toronto, Canada, from 1949 to 1956. Made in 9in (23cm) or 16in (41cm) and 26in (66cm) this cute, fully jointed Teddy with a smiling face and a long topknot is made of brown mohair with contrasting lighter colour chest, inner ears and front paws. The front paws are slightly turned down and the feet are large and flat enabling Punkinhead to stand unaided. The muzzle and feet are velvet.

Reissued in 1986 in a limited edition of 1000 pieces.

PUPPET
(see **Glove Puppet**)

PYJAMA CASE
(see **Novelty**)

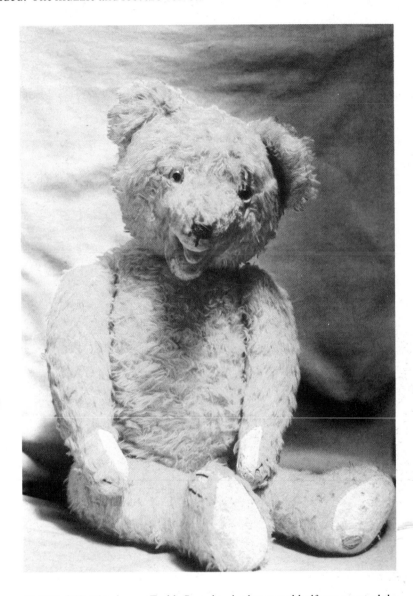

ILLUS. 348. This happy Teddy Bear has had to travel half way around the world before he found someone to love him. Bought in Bitterfeld, Saxony, in East Germany in 1952 as a gift to a little girl in West Berlin from her adoring grandparents on the other side of the Berlin wall. The little girl eventually migrated to Australia, and brought Teddy with her. She sold Teddy in 1988 and told the purchaser that as a little girl she had never liked the bear because she thought that the red open mouth looked like it was bleeding, and she was always frightened of this poor Teddy. This story has a happy ending. Teddy is now part of a large hug and is surrounded by loving Teddy Bears. Teddy is fully jointed, 24in (61cm) tall, excelsior filled, fawn felt paw pads, glass eyes, made from long cotton plush. The open mouth is lined in red felt and has a moulded red felt tongue. Teddy is not marked.

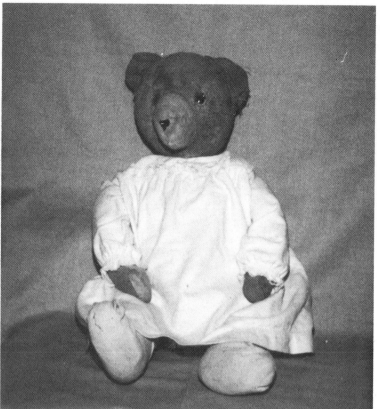

ILLUS. 349. A very brave Teddy Bear, purchased in 1936 in Den Bosch in Holland, she has served as the only toy allowed to six Dutch children during the German occupation of their country. After the war the family migrated to Australia, and again Teddy was called on to help soothe and comfort the children during the upheaval and settling-in period in their new country. Teddy was a very good listener and could understand the children's native language of Dutch! Money was scarce in the new country and so with a new set of paw pads and a pretty new dress she then served another full term as companion to the next generation. 24in (61cm) tall, excelsior filled, fully jointed, she has one eye. Very, very, worn and fragile, her replaced paw pads are worn out, her ears are see-through thin, her muzzle replaced, the fabric around the joints very fragile, but a pair of size 1 all-in-one pyjamas hold her all together. Probably German made. This dear old lady bear now spends her days reclining in a chair and remembering all those years of active duty, both in Holland and then in Australia.

BELOW
ILLUS. 350. This Australian Joy Toys Teddy Bear has been claimed by a second generation. Bought in Melbourne in November 1936 for the cost of one pound (two dollars). Fully jointed, 20in (51cm) tall, large glass eyes, black embroidered claws, mouth, and the distinctive Joy Toys nose. He has had his paw pads replaced so that he can now serve another term as the companion to the original owner's teenage daughter. Photo courtesy Ray Horsey.

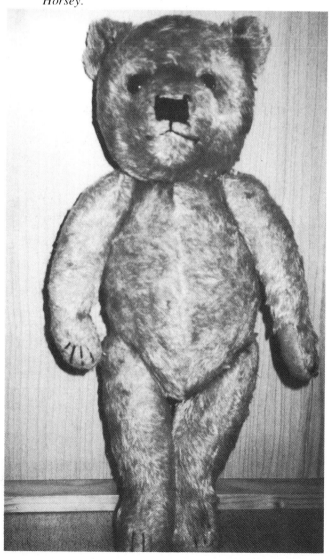

ILLUS. 351. A beautiful Chinese made Teddy Bear pictured with his original owner in 1989. Teddy was bought in 1978 as a "welcome to the world gift" for her.

RAIKES, ROBERT

A Teddy Bear artist who started to make bears in 1983 under the name Mt Shasta Woody Bears. These bears were individually made by Robert Raikes, including the unique carved wooden face.

In 1985 the manufacture of the Raikes' bears was taken over by the Applause Company.

RATTLE

(see **Novelty**)
(see **Noise**)

RELATED ITEMS

The great popularity of Teddy Bear during the early part of this century resulted in many items being made bearing a likeness, to Teddy. It was considered very fashionable by both male and female to wear Teddy Bear jewellery. Tie pins, stick pins, charms, brooches etc, were made from gold, sterling silver and silverplate. Teddy's image decorated personal items such as walking sticks, seals, snuff boxes, pipe sets, desk sets, book marks, boot hooks, handbags, nightwear cases, compacts, cigar cases, and all manner of personal items. More utilitarian items also featured Teddy. Radiator caps for motor vehicles, door knockers, cruet sets, cutlery sets, tea caddy spoons, to name a few.

Babies' rattles and money boxes, made from sterling and silverplate were a popular Teddy Bear decorated item. Chinaware and porcelain items Teddy-decorated (see **China**) were very popular.

Countless firms included Teddy in their advertising (see **Advertising**). Games for adults and children featured pictures of Teddy. Books by the score featuring Teddy as the hero or merely as a decoration were published during this period (see **Storybook Bears**). All of these items are referred to as Related Teddy Bear Items, and are very collectable today by both arctophile and antique collector alike.

ILLUS. 352. A Robert Raikes Teddy Bear made by Applause. This beautiful Teddy is 12in (31cm) tall, fully jointed, made from black synthetic fur fabric. The face and paw pads on the legs are made from wood. The right paw pad is signed by Robert Raikes and numbered 3689 as this beautiful Teddy Bear is a Robert Raikes Club's Collector Bear.

ILLUS. 353. The handle of a walking stick features the head of a bear mounted in a silver ring. c1900. Courtesy David Worland.

ILLUS. 354. A metal half penny token from the 18th century, features a sitting bear. The token reads "Payable by Fletcher and Sharratt". Courtesy David Worland.

ILLUS. 355. A Victorian porcelain pot lid is very collectable. The lid reads "James Atkinson's Bear Grease - 24 Bond Street, London, Price 2/6". A pre-Teddy is pictured wearing a muzzle and chain. Courtesy David Worland.

ILLUS. 356. A ceramic bear advertisement c1890. Courtesy Brian Hill.

ILLUS. 357. A hallmarked sterling silver tea caddy spoon c1930. Courtesy David Worland.

ILLUS. 358. A reversible doll's blanket, 12in (31cm) x 12in (31cm), pink on one side, white on the other. c1920s.

ILLUS. 359. A rare and wonderful sterling silver Teddy Bear seal, hallmarked Birmingham 1909. Courtesy David Worland.

ILLUS . 360. The handle on a set of Teddy Bear cutlery c1912. Marked "Aluminium - Germany". Courtesy Robyn Cox.

ILLUS. 361. A 1907, 9ct gold Teddy Bear watch fob. Courtesy David Worland.

ILLUS. 362. A Teddy Bear pyjama case. The head, limbs and tail are excelsior filled. The torso has a zippered compartment to hold nightwear. English made c1930s.

132

ILLUS. 363. Two tokens for Thorbecke's Cigarettes c1890s. Courtesy David Worland.

ILLUS. 365. A brass pencil top. c1907. Courtesy David Worland.

ILLUS. 366. A silver-plated Teddy Bear rattle c1920. Courtesy Ross Schmidt.

ILLUS. 364. A sterling silver button hook, hallmarked Birmingham 1909. Courtesy David Worland.

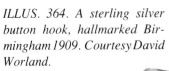

LEFT
ILLUS. 367. A carved wooden bear mounted on a blotter. Courtesy David Worland.

REXINE

A name for oilcloth used for making paw pads on English Teddy Bears during the 1930s, 1940s and 1950s. (see **Paws and Paw Pads**).

133

ILLUS. 368. This silver vesta case features dancing "Roosevelt Bears". c1908. Courtesy David Worland.

ILLUS. 369. A sterling silver Teddy charm hallmarked Chester 1909. Courtesy David Worland.

ILLUS. 371. A silver plated Teddy Bear rattle on a bone teething ring c1908

ILLUS. 370. A brass Teddy Bear motor-cycle mascot c1910. Courtesy David Worland.

RIGHT
ILLUS. 372. A bookmark, hallmarked Birmingham 1926. Courtesy David Worland.

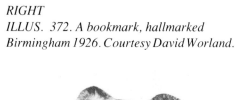

ILLUS. 373. Three rare desk-top inkwells of carved wooden bears all from the first quarter of this century. Courtesy David Worland.

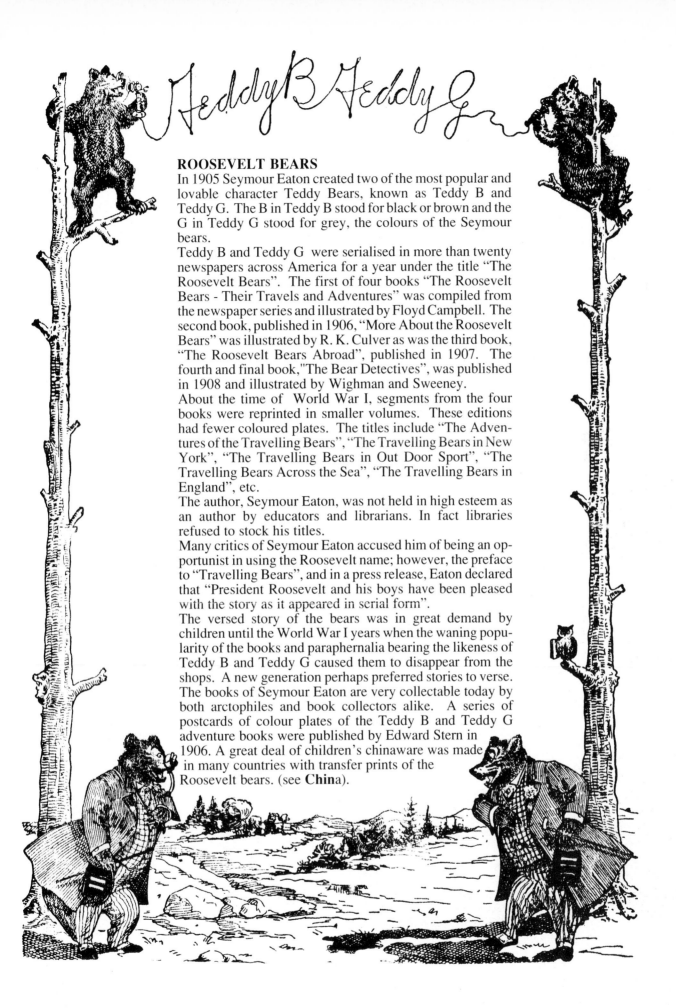

ROOSEVELT BEARS

In 1905 Seymour Eaton created two of the most popular and lovable character Teddy Bears, known as Teddy B and Teddy G. The B in Teddy B stood for black or brown and the G in Teddy G stood for grey, the colours of the Seymour bears.

Teddy B and Teddy G were serialised in more than twenty newspapers across America for a year under the title "The Roosevelt Bears". The first of four books "The Roosevelt Bears - Their Travels and Adventures" was compiled from the newspaper series and illustrated by Floyd Campbell. The second book, published in 1906, "More About the Roosevelt Bears" was illustrated by R. K. Culver as was the third book, "The Roosevelt Bears Abroad", published in 1907. The fourth and final book, "The Bear Detectives", was published in 1908 and illustrated by Wighman and Sweeney.

About the time of World War I, segments from the four books were reprinted in smaller volumes. These editions had fewer coloured plates. The titles include "The Adventures of the Travelling Bears", "The Travelling Bears in New York", "The Travelling Bears in Out Door Sport", "The Travelling Bears Across the Sea", "The Travelling Bears in England", etc.

The author, Seymour Eaton, was not held in high esteem as an author by educators and librarians. In fact libraries refused to stock his titles.

Many critics of Seymour Eaton accused him of being an opportunist in using the Roosevelt name; however, the preface to "Travelling Bears", and in a press release, Eaton declared that "President Roosevelt and his boys have been pleased with the story as it appeared in serial form".

The versed story of the bears was in great demand by children until the World War I years when the waning popularity of the books and paraphernalia bearing the likeness of Teddy B and Teddy G caused them to disappear from the shops. A new generation perhaps preferred stories to verse. The books of Seymour Eaton are very collectable today by both arctophiles and book collectors alike. A series of postcards of colour plates of the Teddy B and Teddy G adventure books were published by Edward Stern in 1906. A great deal of children's chinaware was made in many countries with transfer prints of the Roosevelt bears. (see **Chin**a).

ROOSEVELT, THEODORE
(see "The Beginning")

ROULLET ET DECAMPS
A French firm that made mechanical dolls and toys, including bears. This award-winning firm was in business from 1865-1910 and then from 1910-1921 continued as Decamps Vve and Fils (Decamps Widow and Sons). In 1932 Gaston Decamps from the House of Roullet et Decamps advertised a drinking bear and a dancing bear.

The keys used on Roullet et Decamps mechanical wind-up bears carry the initials "RD" incorporated in the handle of the wind-up key.

Roullet et Decamps bears were usually made of tin and covered in rabbit fur. The dancing bears have large tin-soled feet to enable them to stand. The paws are papier mache.

RUPERT BEAR
A comic strip Teddy Bear created on November 20, 1920 by Mary Tourtel for the Daily Express newspaper in UK; later by artist Alfred Bestall for about forty years. Rupert always wears a red jumper, yellow trousers and scarf with a black check. He has humanised hands and always wears boots. Rupert's image appears on clothing, children's tableware, jewel-

ILLUS. 374. A rare pressed metal lapel pin souvenir of Teddy Roosevelt's visit to Los Angles in 1907. Courtesy David Worland.

lery, furnishings and books.

Rupert Bear books have sold almost 100 million copies world wide. The books vary with soft-cover editions costing a few cents to the hardback colourful yearly annuals. Early editions are now collectable.

Toy Rupert Bears made in Korea are now on the market. These toys are made from white acrylic fur fabric. The red jumper is incorporated into the body structure. The trousers are made separately from the body but are not removable as they are sewn on to the body at the waist. The yellow check scarf is fringed and made separately. The boots are white with black laces. Some Korean made Ruperts have long legs and weighted bottoms.

A very realistic vinyl squeaker toy Rupert Bear was made in the Republic of Ireland. The body is rigid but the head can turn.

Pedigree Toys of UK produced a Rupert in 1960. A flock-covered plaster 2in (5.1cm) Rupert was also produced in the 1960s.

A "Bendy" Rupert was produced in

ILLUS. 376. A mechanical dancing bear made by the French firm of Roullet et Decamps. Made from rabbit fur covered tin with papier mache paws. Note the metal key in the back with the moulded initials R. D.

ILLUS. 375. An early American Teddy Bear wearing a President Roosevelt pin. Courtesy Susan Weiser.

136

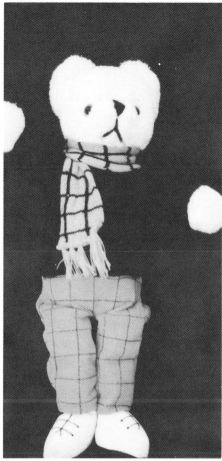

ILLUS. 377. An all original Rupert Bear "Pelham Puppet" Made in England c1950s. Courtesy Ross Schmidt.

ILLUS. 378. This modern Rupert is 12in (31cm) tall, unjointed, the head and front paws are made from white synthetic fur fabric, the costume is incorporated into the body structure. Marked "Rupert - Made in Korea".

ILLUS. 379. An early Rupert Teddy Bear. Maker unknown, but probably English. 14in (36cm) tall, unjointed, the head is excelsior filled, the body is kapok filled, the eyes are glass. The head and paws are mohair fabric, the body is made incorporating the red sweater and checked pants. The scarf is a replacement c1920s. Courtesy Ross Schmidt.

LEFT

ILLUS. 380. Two very realistic Ruperts, both c1960s. The bear on the right is 10 1/2in (26.5cm) tall. Marked on the back "Bendy © 1969. Beaverbrook Newspapers Ltd, Made in Malaysia". He is made of foam rubber over a wire armature that enables him to be posed. The red sweater and checked pants are removable. The scarf is missing and the boots are of painted moulded rubber.

The Rupert on the left is 11 1/2in (29.5cm) tall, made of vinyl with a swivel head. This Rupert is a squeaker toy, the head can be removed to reveal the squeaker hole and "Made in Republic of Ireland" printed on the neck.

1969, made from soft moulded foam rubber over a wire frame. This Rupert is a very good likeness of the drawn Rupert, the head, arms and torso are painted white while the lower body and legs are the unpainted orange foam rubber. This wonderful Rupert has moulded brown boots with black laces and wears a red synthetic plush jumper with yellow and black check cotton pants and scarf. Marked on the back "Bendy © 1969 Beaverbrook Newspapers Ltd, Made in Malaysia".

Burbank Toys produced a Rupert with a pull string voice box that speaks several sentences in a very English accent. This Rupert has the red jumper and yellow checked pants and big brown boots incorporated into the structure of the body. The head is white synthetic plush with a moulded black plastic nose and plastic eyes. This version of Rupert has vinyl human style hands. This very collectable Rupert is tagged to the side seams.

Pelham Puppets of the UK produced a Rupert Bear puppet. The head and hands are made from composition.

At the present time Rupert is being produced under licence from the Daily Express by the Tembro Company of England.

RUSS

The Australian company Russ Berrie and Company, Australia, have been distributors of soft toys since 1979 for the American parent company Russ Berrie.

The range includes baby toys, Teddy Bears, koalas and soft-toy animals.

ILLUS. 381. A Burbank Toys of England Rupert Bear with a pull-string voice box that enables Rupert to speak several sentences in a very British accent. Unjointed, 20in (51cm) tall, Rupert has vinyl humanised hands and a plastic nose. The traditional red sweater and checked yellow and black pants form part of the body structure, the original scarf is missing.

RIGHT
ILLUS. 382. A Russ advertisement c1982. Courtesy Russ Berrie and Co. Aust. P/L.

S

SAMSTAG AND HILDER BROTHERS
(see **Clothes**)

SCHUCO
Schuco is a trademark used by the German company of Schreyer u Co. The company commenced business in 1912 in Nuremburg in Germany. A

ILLUS. 384. A Schuco compact monkey and Teddy Bear. The monkey is c1930s and has paw pads and a flock covered tin face. The Teddy has no paw pads indicating it was made after 1950. On both the monkey and the Teddy the head can be removed, the torso can then be opened to reveal a powder compact. Courtesy Angela Donovan.

ILLUS. 383. The cover of the Schuco 1961 catalogue promoting their Disney-Alweg-System. A mechanical scale model complete with working monorail. Catalogue courtesy Marjory Fainges.

partnership between Adolf Kahn and the founder of the company Heinrich Müller was formed after World War I. The company manufactured Teddy Bears, stuffed toy animals, pull-along toys, ride-on toys and mechanical toys.

Schuco is probably best known for their wonderful miniature Teddies and miniature novelty Teddies (see **Novelty**). The miniature novelty Teddies, made from tin and covered in mohair fabric, include a Yes-No Teddy (see **Yes-No**), a Perfume

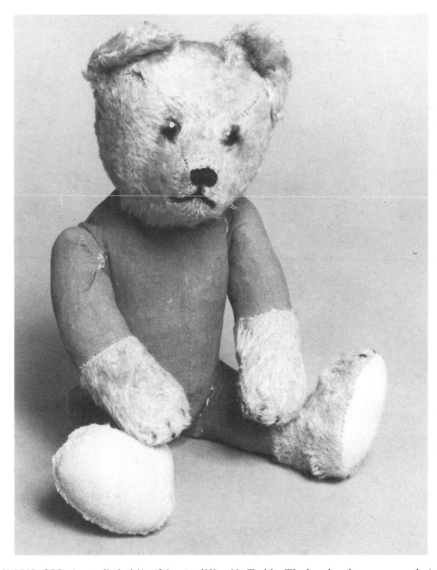

ILLUS. 385. A cute little 14in (36cm) tall Yes/No Teddy. The head and paws are mohair fabric while the torso, legs and arms are made from heavy-weight cotton fabric. This little Teddy has lost her original costume of a cotton print dress and apron. Fully jointed, excelsior filled, clear glass eyes, c1950s. Photograph courtesy Mason Gray Strange Auctions, Sydney.

ILLUS. 386. A page from the 1961 Schuco catalogue. Very few soft toys are included and no Teddy Bears. Catalogue courtesy Marjory Fainges.

Bottle Teddy (the perfume bottle is revealed by removing the bear head), a Compact Teddy (the torso of the Teddy opens to reveal a mirror, a powder compact with powder puff,) and a Tumbling Teddy. Two-faced mini Teddy Bears made by Schuco include a bear with a novelty face with big round eyes and a protruding tongue on one side of the head and a traditional face on the other side of the head. This Teddy was sold under the name of "Janus" (see **Novelty**). Another type of two-faced Teddy had a bisque dolly face on one side of the head and the traditional bear face on the other side.

Mechanical Schuco Teddy Bears were also made in larger sizes. These include a Roller Skating Teddy, an

ILLUS. 387. Three tiny Schuco rabbits found in their original box. Fully jointed, pin-head eyes, embroidered red nose and mouth. No paw pads, felt inner ears, mohair covered tin torsos. They wear their original rayon ribbons. The larger rabbits are 3 1/2in (9cm) tall and the little one is 2 3/4in (7cm) tall. c1960s.

ILLUS. 388. A 14in (36cm) Schuco Teddy Bear, fully jointed, long mohair fabric, short mohair muzzle and feet. Black embroidered nose, mouth and claws, glass eyes, excelsior filled. This Teddy Bear has a concertina music box in his torso. c1940s. Very collectable little Teddy with turned down front paws.

ILLUS. 389. The lid of the Schuco box features pictures of several different types of Teddies as well as other toys. 8in (20cm) long by 4 3/4in (12cm) wide. "Made in Western Germany" is printed on the end of the box in black.

140

Ice Skating Bellhop Teddy, the Tumbling Teddy and a tricycle-riding Teddy (see **Mechanical**). In 1926 Schuco were advertising these miniature novelty Teddies and other toy animals as "Piccolo" toys. Schuco claimed to have sold "more than one million pieces during one year."

The Schuco Teddy Bear, made to the very highest specifications and imaginative designs, is very popular with collectors. A feature of these bears is the cardboard liner in the feet enabling the bear to stand unaided, and the turned-down front paws. The ears are set high on the head, giving the bears an appealing quizzical look. Schuco produced the same type of mechanical and non-mechanical Teddy Bears for many years and determining the age of a Schuco toy can be difficult. However the early Schuco miniature Teddies have felt paw pads while ones manufactured after 1950 have no paw pads. The quality of the fabric used did not appear to deteriorate over the years. Schuco was sold in the late 1950s and was in financial difficulties because of the up and coming Japanese toy industry. Struggling to survive, the great toymaking company of Schuco went bankrupt in 1970.

SCHWARZ F. A. O.

The great American toy retailers, with branches all over the USA and a mail-order business. Have had many "exclusive" lines of Teddy Bears made for them by Teddy manufacturers.

SEALING WAX NOSE

A term used in the Jürgen and Marianne Cieslik book "Button in the Ear, The History of the Teddy Bear and His Friends" to describe the hard moulded material used to make a type of nose found on some early Steiff Teddy Bears (1904-1905) formerly referred to as being made from gutta percha.

SHEEPSKIN
(see **Fabric**)

SHOYER AND COMPANY
(see **Clothes**)

ILLUS. 390. A 12in (31cm) tall Smokey Bear. Unjointed, unmarked, the head, torso, arms and feet top are synthetic brown plush, the muzzle and paws are yellow synthetic plush, the legs and feet bottom are blue denim cotton. This Smokey has lost his hat, he wears a silver plastic ranger badge "Smokey Ranger - Prevent Forest Fires". He also wears a brown plastic belt across the front with a silver plastic buckle that reads "Smokey". The eyes are plastic clip-ins, the nose and tongue are pieces of felt stuck to the muzzle. Maker unknown.

SMOKEY BEAR

The symbol of the cooperative Forest Fire Prevention Organisation of USA.

Smokey first appeared in 1944, drawn by Albert Stoehle, an artist whose work was often on the cover of the "Saturday Evening Post" magazine. Smokey's first appearance was as a true to life bear and then he was depicted wearing jeans.

Smokey is said to have been named after an assistant chief of the New York City Fire Department "Smokey Joe" Martin.

The posters featuring Smokey Bear proved a huge success. In 1946 Rudy Wendelin became Smokey's artist and gave Smokey the cuddly look that is so well known today. In 1950 a forest fire in a New Mexico forest left a badly burnt little orphaned brown bear cub in its wake. After careful fostering the brown bear, now christened "Smokey", survived his ordeal and was presented to the Washington Zoo where he became an immediate star attraction.

In 1952 the "Smokey Bear Act" was passed by Congress, giving the Secretary of Agriculture the authority to grant permission for the use of the Smokey Bear character. A fee now charged for the use of Smokey Bear in advertisements is used for forest fire

ILLUS. 391. Glove puppets of Sooty and his friend Sweep, made by Chad Valley. c1950s. Courtesy Ross Schmidt.

141

prevention.

The first legal Smokey Bear toy was made in 1953 by the Ideal Toy Company of New York. It was made with a vinyl head in a true likeness to the Smokey Bear of the posters. This Smokey carries a blue plastic shovel and wears blue jeans, a belt with a "Smokey" buckle, a hat and ranger badge.

Ideal released the second "Smokey Bear" in 1954. This version of Smokey has a vinyl face and the remainder of the bear is plush.

Knickerbocker Toy Company produced a Smokey in 1968 made from brown synthetic plush with the jeans incorporated into part of the body structure. This Smokey wears a plastic silver ranger badge "Smokey - Ranger - Prevent Forest Fires". A plastic hat and "coonskin tail" complete this bear's costume.

The real Smokey bear died in 1976. The toy Smokey Bears are now considered collectable.

Other different types of Smokeys include a hard plastic version, made in Hong Kong by Tonka and a pull-string Smokey by Knickerbocker.

SOOTY

A glove puppet Teddy from the UK. Now an internationally known mischievous little fellow, he started life in 1949 as a partner to entertainer Harry Corbett. After a guest appearance on television the duo were offered their own show and Sooty went on to become a comic strip character also.

Chad Valley manufactured replicas of Sooty in gold mohair, with black ears, oil cloth paw pads, and plastic eyes.

ILLUS. 392. A rare collection of bear stamps from several different countries. Top row, Sweden, Canada, Greenland, Japan, UK. Middle row, all from USA. Bottom row, all from Australia. Courtesy David Worland.

SQUEAKER

A type of noise maker found in some Teddy Bears, usually used instead of a growler in an effort to cut costs.

Squeakers were fitted into Teddy Bear's torso from the early 1900s and are still used today by soft-toy makers.

Vintage Teddy Bears' squeakers are usually inoperative today.

Many Teddies suffer from a damaged torso due to the squeaker being operated, causing a bald spot and even a torn area.

STAMPS

1979 commemorated The Year of the Child and as part of the celebrations several stamps were issued bearing pictures of Teddy Bears. These included a delightful "Winnie the Pooh" stamp printed in the UK. A stamp from the Isle of Man depicted a chubby little girl holding a beautiful big Teddy Bear.

Many companies produce rubber stamps of Teddy Bears. These are used to decorate stationery among other things.

Steiff used stamps depicting several different scenes for advertising purposes in 1914 and 1920.

STEIFF

In 1847 Margarete Steiff was born in the Black Forest region of what is now West Germany, an area renowned for its toymakers for centuries before Margarete was born.

Confined to a wheelchair from the age of two after an attack of polio which left both of her legs and her right arm paralysed, this industrious lady did not let her infirmities limit her. As an accomplished seamstress, Margarete began making little toy animals from scraps of felt on her hand-driven sewing machine (she and her sister owned the first one in their area!). These she gave to children of friends and relations and the first of these was a little pincushion elephant made in 1880.

This then is the humble beginnings of the great German toy-making firm of Steiff (Margarete Steiff GmbH) of Giengen-an-der-Brenz.

Sooty, Cokey and Sweep were very excited about it because it was a very grand affair, and they washed their faces and brushed their clothes until they were as smart as could be.

They were going to the Ball in Sooty's car so at ten minutes to six Sooty ran outside and lifted the bonnet, and put a penny-in-the-slot.

ILLUS. 393. Sooty and Sweep, in comic strip form. Published by the Daily Mirror. U.K.

ILLUS. 394. Margarete Steiff. Courtesy Steiff.

Margarete's brother Fritz marketed the first Steiff toys at local fairs. The toy-making factory was opened and business thrived. In 1897 one of Margarete's nephews, Richard (later four other nephews, Paul, Otto, Hugo and Ernest would join the company) suggested a new toy line, a bruin. This did not impress Margarete greatly as the bear was to have been made from mohair plush material and not the felt that she had been working in up until then. However Richard had his way. The jointed plush bears were made and taken to the Leipzig Trade Fair in 1903. An American

buyer from the firm of George Borgfeldt and Company saw the little bear and immediately placed an order for 3000; the order then increased to 6000 and by the end of the year the Steiff company had sold 12,000 mohair plush jointed bears. This bear was advertised as Barle. Steiff first used the name Teddy Bear in 1908.

In 1905 the Steiff trademark of the button in the left ear of the toy (Knopf im Ohr) was introduced. The Steiff standard of quality had also been set during this time. No toy left the factory premises without first being inspected by Margarete herself. (This

personal inspection of each toy by a staff member is still maintained to this day).

In 1907 the Steiff firm were employing four hundred factory hands and eighteen hundred "home workers". An American importer, G. C. Poirier, placed an order for more than one hundred different lines at this time. This golden year the Steiff firm named "The Year of the Bear" and sold a record amount of almost one million items for that year. (In 1953 the Golden Anniversary of the Teddy Bear, production was at a quarter of a million items a year and has remained constant each year since then.)

Margarete Steiff died in 1909, aged 62 years. Today Giengen is a company town that supplies the Steiff factory with a large percentage of its workers. The Steiff factory is a well-known spot in this scenic area. The Steiff company has survived in business by changing with the times and it must be remembered that the Steiff company produced wonderfully designed felt dolls as well as Teddy Bears and other toy stuffed animals. In 1912 a branch of Margarete Steiff and Co. Inc. was opened in New York.

At the beginning of World War I in 1914 the production of toys almost came to a halt. In 1916 the company produced goods for the war effort. These included feed bags and gas masks for horses, wooden ammunition boxes and small parts for aeroplanes.

Some toys were made during this difficult period. Paper-plush was used for soft toy making instead of felt (forbidden for the use of anything beside military items) and some wooden toys were made.

Production resumed and continued through the 1920s and 1930s. Many wonderful soft-toy animals, dolls and Teddy Bears were made during this time, both for a home market and for export.

It appears that the shape of the Steiff Teddy changed very little from pre-World War I, say 1914, to the mid 1920s. Photographs from original Steiff catalogues shown in Patricia N. Schoonmaker's "Collector's History of the Teddy Bear" show a 1926 Steiff

Elephant 1904 -1905   *Blank 1904-1905*   *Steiff 1905*   *Painted blue Steiff 1948-1950*   *Blank Blue 1948-1950*   *STEIFF in capital letters 1950*   *Steiff in script 1952*   *Steiff in hollow rivet 1967-1977 present*

ILLUS. 399. Steiff Buttons used on every Steiff Teddy Bear since November 1904. The Steiff metal button-in-ear has changed very little over the years, and it is not possible to accurately date all Steiff Teddies by their buttons as, to quote Steiff "Over the years, these buttons and labels were changed. In certain instances, it is absolutely impossible to give an exact date, since production costs always played an important role and buttons from old stock were often used irrespective of the actual manufacturing date of the product. The use of old and new buttons at the same time has been confirmed mostly for products made in times of crisis."
The cloth tags behind the button were made in white, red and yellow. Until 1981 the material used was cloth-binding linen. From 1980 until 1987 woven cloth, either yellow or white. From 1986 until present day printed on ribbon, either yellow or white.

RIGHT
ILLUS. 400. An early Steiff Teddy Bear c1908. 16in (41cm) tall, gold mohair, shoe-button eyes, excelsior filled, with his button in his ear. Courtesy Christie's Auctions, South Kensington.

ILLUS. 401. A 12in (31cm) Steiff Teddy, fully jointed, excelsior filled, glass eyes. This special Teddy has two Steiff buttons in his ear, both buttons are the same: Steiff with the "F" underlined, 1905-1952.

ILLUS. 402. A close - up of the two buttons in the Steiff Teddy's ear.

with large paws and long limbs. The 1933 version has rounder paw pads and slightly plumper limbs and torso. It was during this period that Steiff produced Mickey and Minnie Mouse. It can be difficult to date Steiff Teddies from this period because of their shape and the fact that with the excep-

ILLUS. 404. An unusual Steiff Teddy Bear, 14in (36cm) tall, shaved muzzle, velvet paw pads, mohair fabric, fully jointed, glass eyes, elongated limbs, black eyes and nose, button in the ear. 1915.

"F" underlined is credited as having been in use during 1940. In 1943 toy-making was forbidden by the authorities and the great Steiff toy factory became a munitions factory.

In 1945 American troops occupied Giengen. A difficult time followed with limited production of toys being sold firstly to the occupying troops only, and then in 1946 for export to America. In 1947 the company was allowed to trade normally and a child's wooden buggy could be purchased if the client could supply Steiff with the materials required to make the buggy (plywood and iron). Production was under way again by 1950 and Teddy Bears were being produced. For a short time some were made with a label stitched into the bear's side seam stating "Made in US Zone, Germany". They also had the traditional ear label and metal button. This company now produces toy Teddy Bears made in accordance to the strict US safety regulations especially for export, and "collector's" Teddy Bears. Reissued replicas of "bears of old", manufactured for the "collector's" market and not as a toy, can be excelsior filled with shoe-button type eyes. The toy Teddy Bears are marked with a yellow cloth ear tag with the metal button. The Teddies that have been re-released for collectors have a white cloth ear tag with the metal button.

Beside the famed factory at Giengen, Steiff also has factories in Austria.

STERNE L. J.
(see **Humphrey B. Bear**)

STRAW FILLED
(See **Excelsior**)

STORYBOOK BEARS
So many story books have been written for children featuring Teddy Bears as the hero. The warm, lovable, sometimes naughty and always almost human little chap is always assured of a wonderful following as he gets in and out of each story book adventure.

Examples of Teddy Bears in literature

include:
Paddington Bear (See **Paddington**)
Roosevelt Bears Teddy B and Teddy G (See **Roosevelt Bear**s)
Rupert Bear (See **Rupert Bea**r)
Sooty (see **Sooty**)

ILLUS. 405. A very adult Teddy Bear from Mrs H. C. Cradock's book "Pamela's Teddy Bears" illustrated by Honor Appleton. c1920s. Published by Thomas Nelson & Sons Ltd.

ILLUS. 403. A 1950s plump Steiff Teddy Bear. Fully jointed, glass eyes, long mohair fabric, felt paw pads, black nose and mouth. The shape of the 1950 bear is much rounder than earlier Teddies.

tion of a few extremely rare examples of a "Bear Head Button", Steiff Teddies had the same designed button from 1905 until 1950. Perhaps a great many Teddies produced between 1920-1940 are credited with being a lot older than they are.

The beginning of World War II in 1939 interrupted production. Cotton plush Teddies were made during this period and a Steiff button without the

ILLUS. 406. This illustration from one of Mrs Cradock's books, "Adventures of a Teddy Bear", illustrated by Joyce L. Brisley. The books in the Teddy Bear series feature a softer, rounder more child-like Teddy, c1949. Published by George G. Harrap and Co. Ltd.

Winnie the Pooh (See **Winnie the Pooh**)

The photographed Teddy Bears in the Dare Wright books, "The Lonely Doll", "The Little One", "Holiday for Edith and the Bears", "The Lonely Doll Learns a Lesson". These beautiful black and white photographs show two Schuco "Yes-No" Teddy Bears and a Steiff Jackie Teddy Bear enjoying many adventures with Edith, an all-felt doll, and Persis, a bisque head, on composition body doll. Published in 1959, 1960, 1961 and 1962 by Oldbourne Book Company Ltd.

Teddy and Teddy Girl from books written by Constance Wickham with pictures by A.E. Kennedy. The books in this series are "Farmyard Folk", "The Teddy Bear Book", "Countryside Folk", "Teddy Bears' Circus", "The Golliwogg Book". First published in 1940 these beautiful picture story books feature a wide-eyed Teddy Bear, Teddy, wearing a collar and tie and a sweet Teddy Girl wearing a red and white check skirt and bow.

The "Little Bear" series of children's books feature a more severe bear. They were written during the 1920s by Frances Margaret Fox with illustrations by Frances Been and Warner Carr. The titles in this series include "Little Bear's Ins and Outs", "Adventures of Sonny Bear", "Doings of a Little Bear", "Little Bear and His Friends", "Little Bear at Work and Play". "Little Bear's Laughing Times", "Little Bear's Playtime", "Little Bear's Ups and Downs". Published by Rand McNally and Company of New York, these books are now considered very collectable. The Reilly and Britten Company of Chicago published a series of eight "The Teddy Bear" books during the early part of the 1900s. Titles included "The Teddy Bears at School", "The Teddy Bears in a Smash-Up" "The Teddy Bears Go Fishing", "The Teddy Bears Come to Life", "The Teddy Bears at the Circus", "The Teddy Bears in Hot Water".

The English publication of the books of Mrs H. C. Cradock written during the 1930s and reprinted into the 1950s are pure delight. Some of the earlier production were illustrated by Honor C. Appleton while later ones were illustrated by Joyce L. Brisley. These tiny hardback books are illustrated in black and white with some of the books having a colour fore page. It is interesting to note how Teddy changes with the times in Mrs Cradock's books. The 1930 Teddies are slimmer, more mature looking, while in the reprinted publication of "The Adventures of a Teddy Bear" Teddy is a chubby, cute wholesome little chap.

Titles in this series include "Adventures of a Teddy Bear", "More Adventures of a Teddy Bear", "Pamela's Teddy Bears".

Teddy Edward, another British Story Book Bear was first written in 1962 by Patrick and Mollie Mathews. The stories are adventures of a little Teddy Bear told in a series of photographs taken by Patrick Mathews while wife Mollie relates the adventures. These books are the same type as the Dare Wright books and have the same charm. Teddy Edward belonged to Sarah Mathews, Patrick and Mollie's youngest daughter, and such was the popularity of this adventuresome little Teddy Bear that a television series has now evolved showing Teddy Edward in exotic locations such as India, Greece and even in the Sahara Desert.

The original Teddy Edward in "Teddy Edward at the Seaside" looks very much like a Chiltern Teddy.

ILLUS. 407. An illustration from "Miss Fluffy Bear's School" by E. Ellsworth, a pre-school reader. c1930. Published by Blackie.

ILLUS. 408. Bobby Bear and his friend Percy Pig. Illustration by Leslie Ellis, published by Dean and Sons Ltd.

However the Teddy Edward in the television series is a much younger Teddy Bear .

The UK's Andy Pandy's Teddy friend has to be included in this section. Never a star in his own right, he was only a supporting member of the Andy Pandy television series and comic strip.

Bobby Bear is another bear that originated in a British comic strip. He first appeared in 1919 as a part of the cast of characters in The Daily Herald comic strip "Playtime". However by the end of 1920, Bobby Bear was a star in his own right with a Bobby Bear Annual on sale in 1922. These annuals continued to be produced well into the 1960s, long after the comic strip had ceased to be. Bobby Bear has several claims to fame, including being drawn by Wilfred Haughton (who also drew the Mickey Mouse Annuals). He was the first bear in British newspapers and had at one time a "Bobby Bear Club" which boasted more than four hundred thousand members.

The annuals of this rather tall, thin (some would say even rat-like) bear with his friends Percy Pig, Maisie Mouse and Ruby Rabbit are now considered collectable by lovers of children's books.

One of the earliest story book bears is the family of Mother, Father and

Baby Bear of the Three Bears fame (see **The Three Bears**). This vintage children's story is as popular today as it was when first written.

"Mishka" (see **Mishka**) is the name given to a bear in Russian folk lore. Mishka has been attributed with many man-like qualities and virtues because of the way he walks upright. Spelled "Misha"(see **Misha**) this Russian favourite was used as the symbol for the 1980 Olympic Games. "Brer Bear", the delightful character in the Uncle Remus books written at

ILLUS. 409. An illustration from the 1947 "The Teddy Bear Book" written by Constance Wickham, illustrated by A. E. Kennedy, published by Wm. Collins and Sons Co. Ltd.

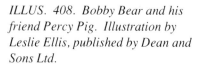

ILLUS. 410. An early children's story book c1905. Courtesy David Worland.

the turn of the century by the American author Joel Chandler Harris, is another humanised lovable bear, a good friend to Brer Rabbit!

SUPER-TED

The Teddy Bear equivalent to Superman. A zip-off bear skin reveals a Super-Ted in a Superman-like costume. Michael Read created this magical bear who is now published in children's story books. The bear designed by Mrs Liz Read was first

ILLUS. 411. A 1940s tracing book.

148

ILLUS. 412. A 1950s tracing book.

manufactured in Wales. However, in 1985, R. Dakin and Company acquired the rights to produce Super-Ted.

The Welsh Super-Ted was a jointed bear, the Dakin version is unjointed. One of the Dakin Super-Teds has a zip-off bearskin while another is made with Super-Ted wearing his "Super" clothes.

The British firm of Bendy make a Super - Ted in moulded foam rubber.

SUSSENGUTH, GEBRUDER

This German company is probably best known for the wonderful "Peter" Bear (see **Peter Bear**). Situated in Neustadt near Coburg, Thuringia, the company manufactured dolls and toys from 1894 up until World War II.

It is very hard to positively identify this maker's bears as they are not tagged. However, known examples appear to be fully jointed, of excellent quality, three black claws on each paw, beige felt paw pads and usually in varicoloured mohair plush.

ILLUS. 413. A 1950s magic pencil book.

ILLUS. 414. A 1950s transfer book.

ILLUS. 415. Super - Ted by R. Dakin and Company, showing him in his bear costume and his Super - Ted costume. Courtesy Australasian Sportsgoods and Toy Retailer.

ILLUS. 416. An illustration from "The Golliwog Book" of Golliwog and Teddy Girl, written by Constance Wickham and illustrated by A. E. Kennedy c1953. Published by Wm. Collins and Sons Co Ltd.

TEDDY BABY

The Steiff company produced a different looking Teddy Bear named Teddy Baby.

Very popular with Teddy lovers Teddy Baby was first produced in the 1930s, and then during the 1950s and re-released in 1984.

This very lovable little Teddy is fully jointed with glass eyes, excelsior filled and has a velvet muzzle, feet and front paw pads and can have an open laughing mouth.

Teddy Baby originally came wearing a red leather collar with a brass bell attached together with a cardboard Teddy Baby tag. The collar has six metal studs and two Steiff buttons. "Teddy Baby" also has a Steiff button in the ear.

ILLUS. 418. An all original mint condition Teddy Baby by Steiff from the 1930s. 7in (18cm) tall, fully jointed, mohair fabric, velvet muzzle, inner mouth, front paw pads and feet, the feet have cardboard liners. Glass eyes, vertically stitched black nose. The paws have air brushed claws, the inner mouth and cheeks are also highlighted in this way. This Teddy Bear wears a red leather collar with six metal studs and two Steiff buttons. Hanging from the collar is a brass bell and the Steiff tag. The tag reads "Teddy Baby ges. gesch. Steiff original marke". A Steiff button is in the left ear.

ILLUS. 417. Two 1930s Steiff Teddy Baby bears. Both are 8in (20cm) tall, fully jointed, glass eyes, open mouth, velvet muzzle, paw pads and feet. Black stitched nose and claws. Courtesy Marvin Cohen Auctions.

TEDDY DOLLS

A toy made of a Teddy Bear's body and a doll's face or head. The faces have been made from bisque, celluloid, composition, metal and later plastic and vinyl. These toys were sometimes made in very distinctive colours and not simply "Teddy Bear" gold. A Royal Blue Teddy Doll has been found with a metal shoulderplate head, marked "Minerva Germany". The Teddy Doll was often advertised as an Eskimo Doll.

"Playthings",the American trade magazine, in 1908 reported that Hahn and Amberg had a wide selection of the "novelty sensation of 1908, the Teddy Doll". These included 8in (20cm) and 10in (25cm) Teddy Dolls with celluloid faces in five colours, 12in (31cm), 13 1/2in (34.5cm), 15in (38cm), 18in (46cm) and 22in (56cm) bisque head with sleep eyes Teddy Dolls in seven colours, and French Teddy Dolls in four sizes in cinnamon colour only with gloves and shoes.

A novelty two-faced Teddy Doll with bisque face and a traditional Teddy face was produced by a German firm in 1914.

In 1912 E. I. Horsman produced a Teddy Doll with a composition "Baby Bumps Can't Break 'Em" head on a jointed plush Teddy Bear body.

One of the rarest of the Teddy Dolls is the Steiff 1907 version. This Teddy Doll has a complete head of felt with glass eyes on a Teddy Bear body.

ILLUS. 419. A celluloid mask face Teddy Doll. 12in (31cm) tall, fully jointed, mohair fabric. Teddy body with felt boots and mittens. (There is a definite similarity between this Teddy Doll and the Gebruder Heubach one). This model was advertised in 1907 at $4.95 a dozen. 151

OPPOSITE PAGE
TOP FAR LEFT
ILLUS. 420 A rare Teddy Doll, approximately 14in (36cm) tall with a fully jointed mohair fabric Teddy body with felt boots and mittens. The bisque head was made by German maker Gebrüder Heubach, a boy's face with moulded hair, closed mouth and intaglio eyes. The head is complete, the fabric creates a hood around the back of the head and is topped off with a silk bow. Courtesy Angela Donovan.

CENTRE
ILLUS. 421. A close-up of the head of the Gebruder Heubach Teddy Doll.

TOP NEAR LEFT
ILLUS. 422. A very sweet Teddy Doll with a German bisque head. Fully jointed mohair fabric body, excelsior filled. The front paws are felt, the head has an open mouth and glass eyes. No visible marks. Courtesy Dot Gillett.

BOTTOM FAR LEFT
ILLUS. 423. A rare possum-doll 7in (18cm) tall, fully jointed with a long tail, made of mohair fabric, excelsior filled. The German bisque doll head is situated under the head, in the neck. The possum head has shoe-button eyes and a nose and ears. Courtesy Dot Gillett.

BOTTOM NEAR LEFT
ILLUS. 424. An unusual Teddy Doll from the 1950s. 17in (43cm) tall, fully jointed, excelsior filled, long cotton plush fabric, check chenille paw pads. The feet have cardboard linings to enable this Teddy Doll to stand unaided. The large ears are wire lined. The face is a vinyl mask, well moulded with curls around the forehead. Unmarked.

ILLUS. 425. A Shackman of New York, Small Bear School. The school consists of six desks and seats fixed to a floor, a teacher's desk, complete with red apple and a chalk board and stand, all made from wood. The six pupils are identical 2 1/2in (6.5cm) tall and marked with an oval sticker "Made in Poland". They have jointed limbs, pin-head eyes and a pink rayon bow. The fabric is gold synthetic and they are excelsior filled. Teacher is not marked and is not the same as the pupils, 4in (10cm) tall, jointed limbs, pin-head eyes, synthetic plush fabric, excelsior filled and a red rayon bow. It is hard to find these schools so complete.

ILLUS. 426. The box of the Shackman Teddy school set.

TEDDY EDWARD
(See **Storybook Bears**)

TEDDY SCHOOL

This term refers to a group of student's desks together with a larger desk for the teacher and a chalkboard, the pupils and teacher being tiny Teddy Bears.

The American company of Shackman released a boxed Teddy School in the 1970s. This set comprised six table type desks and chairs mounted on a wood base, a larger desk and chair for the teacher. Teacher's desk has a red wooden apple fixed to it. A chalkboard and tiny book make up the set. One type of Shackman Teddy

School has six 2 1/2in (6.5cm) tall Polish Teddy Bear pupils and a 4in (10cm) tall Japanese-made teacher while another set may have Japanese-made pupils and teacher. This Shackman Teddy School was discontinued in 1980.

Gebr. Hermann K G released a Teddy School in 1986 to celebrate their 75th anniversary.

This set consists of a Teddy Bear school teacher 14in (35.6cm) tall and six Teddy Bear pupils 8in (20.3cm) tall. All of these Teddies are dressed.

ILLUS. 427. The "Nostalgic Teddy School" by Hermann. Each set is made up of fifteen pieces of furniture, a teacher 13 1/2in (35cm) tall, six pupils 8in (20cm) tall, two satchels and two canes. A top quality set, each Teddy is made of the highest quality mohair fabric and beautifully dressed. Courtesy Gebr. Hermann. KG

Six combined desks and seats, a teacher's desk, a chalkboard and pointer. This set was still on the market in 1989.

TEDDY TURNOVER
(See **Topsy Turvy Teddy**)

THE THREE BEARS
The first version of this popular fairy story was written in 1831 by Eleanor Mure (1799-1885) as a gift to her nephew on his fourth birthday.

The story has changed over the years, becoming more gentle. The original "Three Bears" featured an old witch, who was later replaced by a golden haired little girl.

In 1837 an edited version of Eleanor Mure's "The Three Bears" appeared in print, written by Robert Southey. This version still retained the old witch as the interloper into the home of the three male bears.

In 1850 a little girl by the name of Silverhair was introduced into the story written by Joseph Cundall.

In 1852 the version written by Frances Elizabeth Barrows still has the old witch and the three male bears. However the accompanying picture shows the three bears as a family of Father, Mother and Baby.

By 1888 a McLoughlin Company, USA, publication of "The Three Bears" features Goldilocks and the family of bears. This is thought to be the first publication featuring the story of the Three Bears as we know it today.

Every year new publications of this old favourite appear on the market and even after 156 years this beloved fairy story is still popular.

ILLUS. 429. "Three Bears Porridge". A linen bag of flaked oatmeal sold by Jas. F. McKenzie and Co. Pty Ltd, Melbourne, Sydney, Brisbane, Fremantle. c1900.

ILLUS. 430. A set of cut and sew Three Bears by Cranston Print Works, VIP Fabrics. c1977. Courtesy Christine Johnson.

ILLUS. 431. The Three Bears from an English story book c1916.

ILLUS. 428. The reverse side of the McKenzie porridge bag.

ILLUS. 432. A Spear's Sewing Card game features the Three Bears c1910.

"But the Baby Bear said,
'Nothing ever was sweeter.'"

ILLUS. 433. An illustration from Silver Locks and the Bears c1877, by Mrs Bates and Mrs Finley. Courtesy David Worland.

ILLUS. 435. The cover of the Mrs Bates and Mrs Finley version of Silver Locks and the Bears. c1877. Courtesy David Worland.

ILLUS. 434. The Three Bears by Leslie Brookes. The little girl is called Goldenlocks, the bears are called the little, small, wee bear, the middle bear and the great, huge bear. c1900.

RIGHT
ILLUS. 437. The Three Bears from an English story book c1916.

ILLUS. 436. The Three Bears by Leslie Brookes

Cheap Animals
of cotton
Animaux en coton
á prix modérés

Cats, dogs, and rabbits in grey 5% cheaper
Chats, chiens et lapins en coton gris à 5%
meilleur marché.

dz 8

size-number — numéro de grandeur No.	without voice sans voix 1 030	2 045	3 070	4 090	5 110	6 150	7 200	8 200
		with voice — avec voix						
Cat lying white — chat couché, blanc . . No. 140w	1.40	1.85	2.15	2.50	3.05	3.90	4.60	5.55
piece weight — poids par pièce abt./env. gr.								
Rabbit lying white — lapins couché, blanc . No. 141w	1.65	1.90	2.30	2.65	3.15	4.10	4.85	5.80
piece weight — poids par pièce abt./env. gr.								
Dog lyng white — chien chouché, blanc . No. 152w	1.65	1.90	2.30	2.65	3.15	4.10	4.85	5.80
piece weight — poids par pièce abt./env. gr.								
Dog sitting white — chien assis, blanc . No. 146w	2.-	2.35	2.70	3.30	4.20	5.-	6.-	
piece weight — poids par pièce abt./env. gr.								
Dog standing white — chien debout, blanc . No. 156w	2.-	2.35	2.70	3.30	4.20	5.-	6.-	
piece weight — poids par pièce abt./env. gr.								
do. on wheels — monté sur rues . No. 2156w		2.40	2.80	3.20	3.75	4.70	5.50	6.50
piece weight — poids par pièce abt./env. gr.								
Elephant — éléphant . . . . No. 170			2.45	3.-	3.75	4.70	6.10	7.25
piece weight — poins par pièce abt./env. gr.								
do. on wheels — monté sur roues . No. 2170			2.90	3.45	4.25	5.20	6.60	8.25
piece weight — poids par pièce abt./env. gr.								
Donkey — âne . . . . . No. 144			2.70	3.10	3.75	4.65	5.85	7.40
piece weight — poids par pièce abt./env. gr.								
do. on wheels — montés sur roues . No. 2144			3.10	3.55	4.25	5.15	6.40	7.90

Mechanical Tumbling figures — Culbuteurs mécaniques.

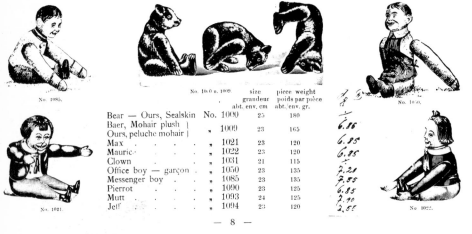

	No. 1000 u. 1009.	size grandeur abt. env. cm	piece weight poids par pièce abt./env. gr.	
Bear — Ours, Sealskin	No. 1000	25	180	
Baer, Mohair plush } Ours, peluche mohair }	„ 1009	23	165	6.15
Max	„ 1021	23	120	6.85
Maurice	„ 1022	23	120	6.85
Clown	„ 1031	21	115	
Office boy — garçon .	„ 1050	23	135	7.20
Messenger boy .	„ 1085	23	135	7.55
Pierrot	„ 1090	23	125	6.85
Mutt	„ 1093	24	125	7.90
Jeff	„ 1094	23	120	7.55

No. 1085.   No. 1000.   No. 1021.   No. 1022.

— 8 —

ILLUS. 438. A page from an early trade magazine, advertising "Mechanical tumbling figures, including figures of bears, Max and Maurice, office boy and messenger boy." Maker unknown. c1913.

*LEFT
ILLUS. 439. A 13 1/2in (34cm) rare Steiff somersaulting Teddy Bear c1910. Fully jointed, mohair fabric, shoe-button eyes. This mechanical Teddy is operated by winding his arms. Courtesy Sotheby's Auctions, London.*

TOPSY TURVY TEDDY
A topsy turvy doll is a toy made from two dolls without legs joined at the torso. The dolls are usually contrasting and can be a black and white doll or a smiling and crying doll. A skirt usually hides one of the dolls. A topsy turvy Teddy has a doll at one end and a Teddy Bear at the other, joined at the torso.

The trade magazine of the USA, Playthings, in 1907 reported that "The Dreamland Doll Company of the USA made a 13in (33cm) topsy turvy toy Sandy Andy and Teddy Turnover, with a cloth doll at one end and a Teddy Bear at the other separated by a reversible skirt."

The Teddy Bear has a jointed head and arms and is made from gold mohair plush while the doll is lithographed.

TOYLAND LTD
Israeli manufacturers of soft toys, including Teddy Bears, for the home market and export.

TRICKY
A Yes-No toy including Teddy Bears released by Schuco in 1950.   5in (13cm) tall, mohair fabric over tin, tagged "Made in US Zone, Germany - D.B. Pat. Ang. Int. Patents Pending" on one side and "Schuco - Tricky - Patents Ang." on the other.

TUMBLING TEDDIES
(See **Mechanical**)

TWO FACED
(See **Novelty**)
(See **Teddy Doll**s)

TWYFORD
An English company situated in London. Has been making quality jointed Teddy Bears since the 1930s. One of the distinctive features of these bears is the red felt paw pads. Label reads "Twyford Product, Made in England, Action Toycraft Ltd, London W3". It is believed that Twyford was a subsidiary company of J. K. Farnell.

U

UNIDENTIFIED

Usually the maker of most unmarked Teddy Bears remains unknown and Teddy remains unidentified. The largest percentage of old bears are sold "Maker Unknown" or "Maker thought to be...".

9 1/2in (24cm) tall, fully jointed, shoe-button eyes, black embroidered nose and mouth, gold mohair. No paw pads or claws. c1910. Courtesy L. Albright.

18in (46cm) tall, fully jointed, two coloured gold and brown tipped mohair fabric, a very large head in proportion to the rest of the body. Excelsior filled, real leather paw pads, glass eyes, large ears, black nose and mouth, no claws.

14in (36cm) tall, fully jointed blue mohair, excelsior filled, very large glass eyes, felt paw pads, well defined nose. The mouth, nose and large claws embroidered in black.

22 1/2in (57cm) tall, fully jointed, glass eyes, well defined hump. Courtesy Ross Schmidt.

16in (41cm) tall, fully jointed, soft filled, rexine paw pads, glass eyes, shapeless limbs, very large black claws, almost round head, gold mohair.

14in (36cm) tall, two coloured brown and gold tipped mohair fabric, fully jointed, felt paw pads, large clear glass eyes with black pupils, squat baby shape.

LEFT
14in (36cm) tall, fully jointed, excelsior filled, shoe-button eyes, gold mohair fabric, probably c1910.
Courtesy L. Albright.

ILLUS. 440. A hug of unidentified Teddies, unmarked and maker unknown. This does not make these Teddies less collectable - but does make them less valuable.

However it is possible to identify the maker of some unmarked Teddy Bears by the characteristics they share with marked bears of the same maker.

Some Steiff, Alpha Farnell, Knickerbocker, Hermann, Emil, and Schuco Teddies to name a few can be positively identified in some cases as a particular style is unique to a particular manufacturer.

The positive identification of most unmarked Teddies will never be achieved.

UNMARKED TEDDY BEARS

Most vintage Teddy Bears are unmarked with a maker's label or tag. There are several reasons for this, including:

Many cloth tags that were attached to a Teddy were sewn into seams in such a way that it is a very simple thing to remove them, as in most cases the labels and tags are held in place by only three or four stitches.

Some cloth tags that have remained on Teddy until today have faded to such a degree that it is impossible to read any manufacturer's name.

Mothers of young children often removed Teddy's cloth tags or labels as a safety measure against them being eaten by the young owners.

Most German-made Teddy Bears were made by outworkers in a cottage industry situation who then sold their finished Teddies to the firm that had ordered them, or in some cases, to the highest bidder. These bears were then tagged with a cardboard swing tag carrying the name of the distributor. More than 90% of all Teddy Bears made in Germany before 1975 were marked (or unmarked) in this manner. The exceptions to this are the companies of Steiff and Petz and perhaps one or two other companies.

Unmarked Teddy Bears usually do not bring as much money as a Teddy complete with a readable manufacturer's label or tag.

US ZONE

At the end of World War II, in 1945 Germany was divided into four zones. The Russian Zone became East Germany. The remaining three zones under the control of Great Britain, USA and France became West Germany, and the demarcation line separating East from West became known as the Iron Curtain. Very little toy making took place in Germany during the early

ILLUS. 442. A close-up of the US Zone tag.

part of the war (1939-42) and by early 1943 toy making was forbidden completely by the government.

The US Zone in Germany held many of the factories that had, up until the war, produced dolls and toys (this included Giengen where the Steiff factory is located).

By 1947, limited production of toys and dolls was being undertaken by some of these factories, including Steiff. The toys and dolls, including Teddy Bears, were then marked "Made in US Zone Germany".

This mark was generally discontinued in the 1950s and replaced with "Made in West Germany".

ILLUS. 441. Unmarked Teddy Bear, but definitely a Merrythought. 20in (51cm) tall, soft filled, glass eyes. Mouth, nose and claws embroidered in black. Tag is missing from right foot.

ILLUS. 443. Unmarked Teddy Bear by Chiltern. 14in (36cm) tall, fully jointed, kapok filled, rexine paw pads, moulded plastic nose.

ILLUS. 444. The maker of this little Teddy is unknown even though he is tagged Baren Bier. Jointed limbs, glass eyes, synthetic fabric. This type of little bear could be mistaken for Japanese made Teddies. Courtesy Ross Schmidt.

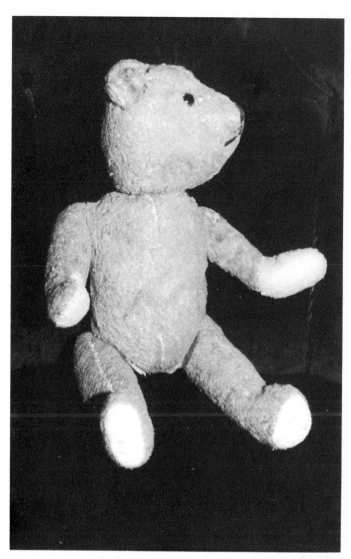

ILLUS. 445. 12in (31cm) tall, German Teddy, made of gold cotton flock, felt paw pads, fully jointed, glass eyes, black embroidered nose and mouth, no claws. Squeaker in the torso. Tagged on the right foot "Made in US Zone, Germany". White cotton tag with black printing.

ILLUS. 446. This Teddy Bear is 20in (51cm) tall, fully jointed, glass eyes, excelsior filled, gold cotton plush with fawn felt paw pads. Black embroidered mouth and nose, no claws. Tagged to the right foot with a heavyweight cotton tag printed in black ink "Made in US Zone, Germany".

ILLUS. 447. A 9in (30cm) unmarked Teddy c1956 by Steiff. Courtesy L. Albright.

ILLUS. 448. An unmarked Teddy, the maker unknown. 10in (25cm) tall, fully jointed, although his head has been sewn on to his body, tiny shoe-button eyes, excelsior filled. He has no paw pads and is almost completely bald. An early little Teddy with a lot of appeal.

ILLUS. 449. A rare bear. 24in (61cm) tall. Unnmarked and maker unknown. Made from gold mohair skin. Glass eyes, fully jointed, paw pads are made from brown leather. This beautiful quality Teddy Bear is filled with a mixture of excelsior and raw greasy wool. The quality of this lovely Teddy is excellent. c1930. Courtesy Debra Aldridge.

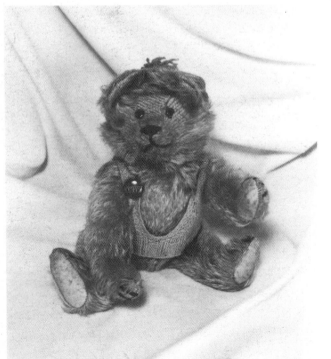

ILLUS. 450. An unmarked Teddy with very long mohair fabric. 13in (32cm) tall, fully jointed, glass eyes, excelsior filled. Black embroidered nose, mouth and claws. Paw pads are felt. c1913. Courtesy L. Albright.

ILLUS. 451. An unmarked Teddy standing on all four legs. Excelsior filled, glass eyes, gold mohair fabric, black embroidered nose and mouth. c1920s.

EARLY
TO BED
EARLY
TO RISE

BED TIME STORIES

ILLUS. 456. A beautiful colour plate from the Wickham and Kennedy book "The Teddy Bear Book" c1947. Published by Wm. Collins and Sons Co. Ltd.

LEFT
ILLUS. 457. This very pugnacious Teddy Bear has his original
blue eyes. Fully jointed, gold mohair fabric, excelsior filled,
rexine paw pads. 21in (53cm) tall. Probably English made,
c1930s.

BOTTOM LEFT
ILLUS. 458. This sweet baby bear is unmarked but is probably
by Joy Toys. Jointed limbs, gold mohair, excelsior and kapok
filled, felt paw pads, glass eyes. The front paws are upturned
and the neck is unjointed. c1950s.

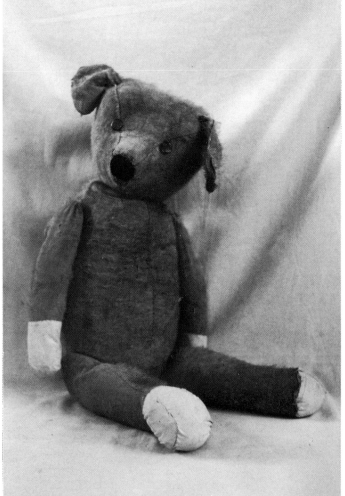

ILLUS. 459. A large old Teddy Bear with replaced eyes, nose and
paw pads. Excelsior filled, fully jointed, very little shaping to the
limbs. The ears of this Teddy have been cut into the head. Probably
German made, c1930. Courtesy Marjory Fainges.

ILLUS. 460. An unmarked brown plush Teddy Bear by Steiff, 26in (65cm) tall, fully jointed, shoe-button eyes, felt paw pads. His button is missing but he is definitely a Steiff Teddy. Courtesy Christie's Auctions, South Kensington.

ILLUS. 461. A sweet faced Teddy Bear, unmarked but probably English. 12in (30cm) tall, fully jointed, mohair fabric, soft filling, velvet paw pads, black embroidered nose, mouth and claws. Courtesy L. Albright.

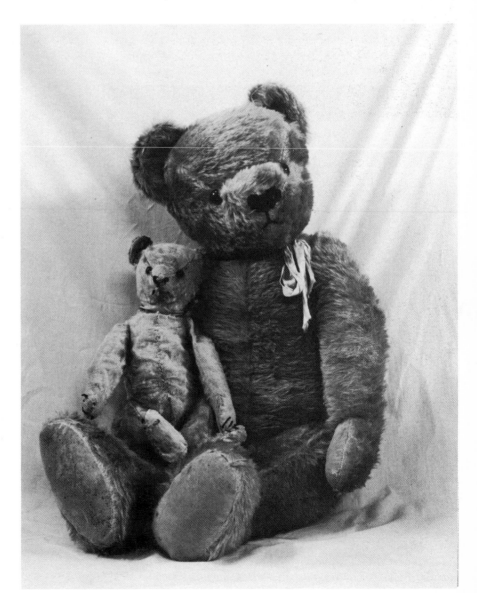

RIGHT
ILLUS. 462. Two unmarked Teddies, makers unknown. The larger is English made, c1940, gold mohair fabric with suedette paw pads, glass eyes and soft filling. The little chap is German made, excelsior filled with shoe-button eyes. c1910. Courtesy Marjory Fainges.

ILLUS. 463. A beautiful illustration from Fredrika Grosvenor's book "A Very Small Tale of Two Very Small Bears". Published by McLoughlin Bros., of New York, 1905. Courtesy David Worland.

ILLUS. 464. Covers from two Bobby Bear Annuals, left c1940, right c1960. Note the chubbier, rounder Bobby on the cover of the 1960 annual. Published in Great Britain by Dean and Sons Ltd.

ILLUS. 465. Coloured Lantern Slides from a Primus Junior Lecturer's Series "The Three Bears." c1900.

ILLUS. 466. An unmarked Chad Valley Teddy Bear. 16in (40cm) tall, fully jointed, gold mohair fabric with velvet paw pads, kapok filled, and glass eyes. This Teddy has the broad head and the overly large nose typical of a Chad Valley Teddy, c1950.

ILLUS. 467. An unusual looking Teddy Bear, not marked but of English origin. Gold mohair fabric, kapok filling, large glass eyes, fully jointed. The paw pads are replaced on his chunky limbs. c1930.

LEFT
ILLUS. 468. A 12in (30cm) rare unmarked musical Teddy with a concertina-ype action music box in his torso. Yellow mohair fabric, fully jointed, large glass eyes, felt paw pads, shaved muzzle. Courtesy Marvin Cohen Auctions.

OPPOSITE PAGE BOTTOM LEFT
ILLUS. 469. An unmarked Teddy, maker unknown. 14in (35cm) tall fully jointed, long mohair fabric, excelsior filled, glass eyes, black embroidered nose, mouth and claws, felt paw pads. This unusual Teddy is thought to be German made, c1920.

OPPOSITE PAGE BOTTOM RIGHT
ILLUS. 470. A very worn early Merrythought Teddy. Fully jointed, large glass eyes. He has the remains of his nose and distinctive wrap-around claws, c1930s.

168

ILLUS. 471. A hug of early Teddies. From left to right, 12in (30cm) fully jointed with mohair fabric and shoe-button eyes. 18in (45cm) white mohair Teddy with shoe-button eyes. 14in (35cm) Steiff Teddy Bear, champagne colour, fully jointed, shoe-button eyes. 12in (30cm) Steiff Teddy Bear with gold mohair fabric, shoe-button eyes. Only the champagne coloured Steiff is marked with his identifying button. Courtesy Marvin Cohen Auctions.

ILLUS. 472. A 40in (102cm) bisque head Jumeau doll teacher shows her pupils the three Rs. To the left, a 20in (51cm) tall Joy Toys Teddy c1930s is helping a 24in (61cm) tall unmarked Teddy with his writing slope. Opposite sits a 40in (102cm) Chiltern Teddy Bear who is having no trouble reading his ABCs, the little fellow who looks too small to go to school is a 1910 Alpha Farnell Teddy, 20in (51cm) tall. The puppy is a 1920 clutch purse with the opening in his back. Teddies are sitting at a rare Australian colonial pine settle-type desk c1835. The Chiltern Teddy, courtesy Helen Jones.

A. *This view shows Teddy Turnover, jointed arms and head, excelsior filled, shoe-button eyes. The original red skirt hides the cloth doll.*

B. *The cloth doll in her original red dress, the skirt is hiding Teddy.*

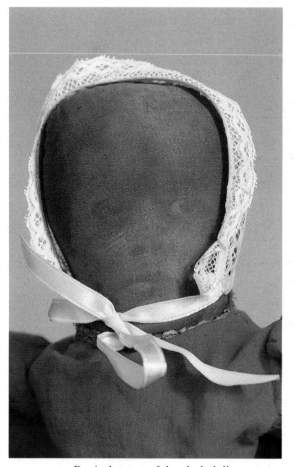

C. *A close-up of Teddy.*

D. *A close-up of the cloth doll.*

ILLUS. 473. *The Topsy Turvy Teddy, 13in (33cm) tall, one end of this very collectable toy is a Teddy Bear, the other is a cloth doll, joined in the middle. Courtesy Angela Donovan.*

ILLUS. 474. c1910 Courtesy N.S.W. State Library.

V

VERNA

An Australian company that commenced doll making in 1941 in Victoria. The company changed hands in 1948 and a larger variety of dolls and toys, including Teddy Bears, were manufactured until the mid-1980s. Initially Verna Teddies were made from top quality mohair fabric with glass eyes, and were fully jointed and filled with excelsior and cotton flock. From the 1960s the Verna Teddy was filled with foam rubber.

One version of the Verna Teddy has a very square shaped muzzle and one type of 1960s Verna Teddy has a black piece of felt sewn into place as a nose. This type of Teddy has plastic eyes.

Verna Teddies were tagged with a white cloth tag bent double with both ends sewn into the seam and "Verna, Made in Australia" printed in red.

ILLUS. 475. The Verna tag used in 1950-1970, "Verna Made in Australia".

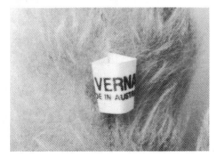

ILLUS. 478. The Verna tag in use in the 1980s. "Verna Made in Australia".

VOICE BOX

This term usually refers to Teddy's growler or squeaker (See **Growler**) (See **Squeaker**) (See **Noise**).

ILLUS. 476. A 1980s Verna Teddy. Unjointed, plastic eyes and nose, red felt tongue, synthetic plush. Contrasting paws and inner ears. Tagged to the inside left leg.

ILLUS. 477. A 1960s Verna Teddy. Fully jointed, soft filled, glass eyes, vinyl paw pads, felt nose. Tagged to the left side seam.

ILLUS. 479. Courtesy Australasian Sportsgoods and Toy Retailer, September 1982.

ILLUS. 481. Two Hermann Zotty Teddy Bears. Beautiful quality, dual coloured long mohair, felt peach coloured paw pads and inner mouth. Short mohair muzzles, glass eyes, fully jointed. The nose, mouth and long claws are embroidered in black. These two very collectable Teddies feature the turned-down front paw pads. The larger Zotty is 11in (28cm) tall, the smaller 8in (20cm) tall. c1950s.

ILLUS. 480. An impressive Verna Teddy. This type has the very square muzzle. Fully jointed, glass eyes, soft filled c1950s.

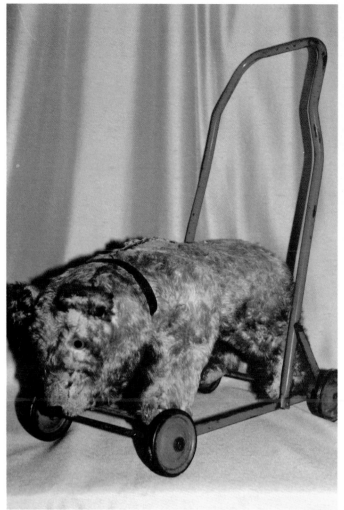

ILLUS. 482. A Chiltern push-along bear on wheels. This mohair fabric covered bear is excelsior filled over a steel frame on a steel chassis. The metal wheels have rubber tyres. The bear has glass eyes and a flat back from years of faithful service. 15in (38cm) long by 8in (20cm) tall. c1950s.

ILLUS. 483. A Victorian lamb on wheels. The wheels are mounted onto a platform. The lamb is sheepskin covered carton with wooden legs and glass eyes. 12in (31cm) long by 12in (31cm) tall. By pushing down on the nose of the lamb a voice mechanism in the neck is activated. c1900.

RIGHT.
ILLUS. 484. An unusual bear on wheels, made of fur fabric covered hollow carton. Shoe-button eyes, hump back, metal axles with red wooden wheels. This interesting bear has an eyelet in his chest, possibly to activate a voice box. The bear is unmarked 11in (28cm) tall, and 16in (41cm) long.

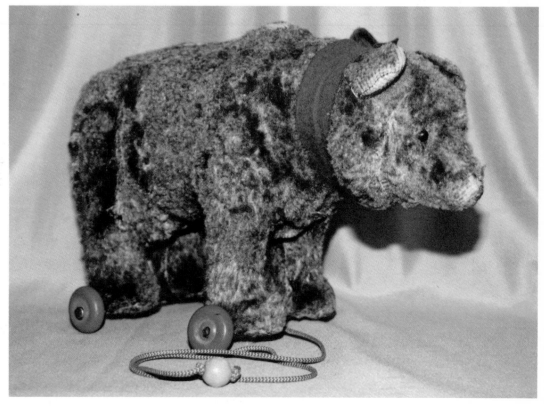

ILLUS. 485. **A sturdy friend.** Courtesy N.S.W. State Library.

W

WHEELS

Most manufacturers of soft toys have manufactured toys on wheels. These toys can depict many different birds and animals, including horses, sheep, cows, lions, cats, dogs, camels, rabbits, ducks, elephants, donkeys, pigs, deer, monkeys, ostriches, goats and bears.

| No. 4490/5. | 16 ins. long | 14 ins. high | ... | 6/6 each |
| No. 4490/6. | 19 ins. „ | 16 ins „ | „ | 10/6 „ |

ILLUS. 486. An advertisement in a catalogue from Faudels Ltd., London, c1912. A muzzled bear on wheels.

Toy Department.

GRACE BROS. THE MODEL STORE. BROADWAY. SYDNEY.

ILLUS. 487. Wheeled toys have always been popular. This advertisement from 1908 shows eight different toy animals on wheels. Courtesy Grace Bros., Sydney.

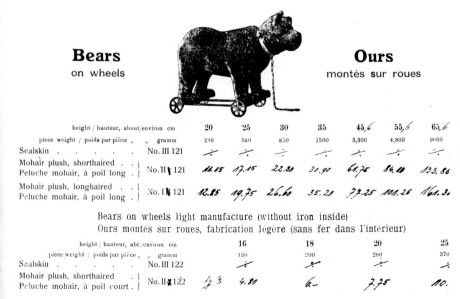

	Bears on wheels				**Ours** montés sur roues		
height / hauteur, about/environ cm	20	25	30	35	45,6	55,6	65,6
piece weight / poids par pièce „ „ gramm	230	560	850	1500	3,800	4,800	9000
Sealskin . . . . . No. III 121	∴	∴	∴	∴	∴	∴	∴
Mohair plush, shorthaired . . Peluche mohair, à poil long . No. II 121	14.15	17.15	22.30	30.90	61.75	84.10	133.86
Mohair plush, longhaired . . Peluche mohair, à poil long . No. I 121	12.85	19.75	26.60	35.20	73.25	101.25	161.30

Bears on wheels light manufacture (without iron inside)
Ours montés sur roues, fabrication légère (sans fer dans l'intérieur)

		16	18	20	25
height / hauteur, abt./environ cm		16	18	20	25
piece weight / poids par pièce „ „ gramm		130	200	280	370
Sealskin	No. III 122	∴	∴	∴	∴
Mohair plush, shorthaired . Peluche mohair, à poil court .	No. II 122	4.3 4.80	6.—	7.75	10.—

ILLUS. 488. A page from a soft toy catalogue, maker unknown. Note the extraordinary similarity between this bear and the bear in the photograph on page 176.

There are several types of wheeled bears. Those on a chassis, usually built of metal, carry the bear and the wheels are on axles. In others, the wheels are attached directly to the bear's feet. Yet another is the platform type with the bear standing on a wooden platform with wheels fitted to axles beneath the platform. Wheeled bears can be ride-on, pull-along or push-along toys.

Always popular with children, wheeled toys, including bears, have been made for centuries.

Very few Teddy Bears on wheels have been made. However from 1913 the Steiff company manufactured a Teddy Bear sitting on a chassis. It was known as Record Teddy. In 1926 a clockwork version was made.

Probably the cutest Teddy Bear on wheels was made by Steiff in 1939, a pull-along baby Teddy lying on his back holding a bell in each hand.

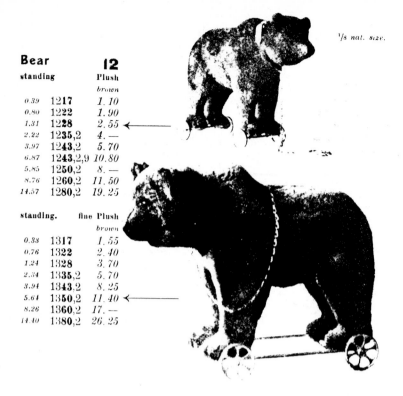

1/8 nat. size.

Bear   **12**

standing		Plush brown
0.39	1217	1.10
0.80	1222	1.90
1.31	1228	2.55 ←
2.22	1235,2	4.—
3.97	1243,2	5.70
6.87	1243,2,9	10.80
5.85	1250,2	8.—
8.76	1260,2	11.50
14.57	1280,2	19.25

standing.		fine Plush brown
0.38	1317	1.55
0.76	1322	2.40
1.24	1328	3.70
2.34	1335,2	5.70
3.94	1343,2	8.25
5.64	1350,2	11.40 ←
8.26	1360,2	17.—
14.40	1380,2	26.25

ILLUS. 489. A bear on wheels advertised by Steiff in 1913.

ILLUS. 490. Pooh Bear waits for 4 o'clock.

ILLUS..491. The Chiltern tag found on the underside of the push-along bear on page 175.

WINNIE THE POOH

This very famous English character Teddy Bear was created by A.A. Milne in the 1920s. The story book "Winnie the Pooh" is said to have been based on an Alpha Farnell Teddy Bear bought from Harrods in London for Milne's son Christopher Robin. The wonderful adventures of the little bear and his friend Piglet, Tigger and Eeyore have thrilled children all over the world for more than sixty years.

Many companies have made toy Winnie the Pooh bears including one made for Disneyland in USA. Richard Wright, a modern doll and bear artist has produced a very realistic Winnie the Pooh in recent years. Gund (See **Gund**) has released several versions for the department store Sears in USA. During the 1970s The House of Metti, a South Australian firm, produced a Walt Disney soft vinyl jointed Winnie the Pooh.

ILLUS. 492. These two Winnie the Pooh bears were made almost twenty years apart. The little bear was bought from Disneyland in the early 1980s, while his big friend was also bought in America but in the 1960s. Courtesy Janine Gibson.

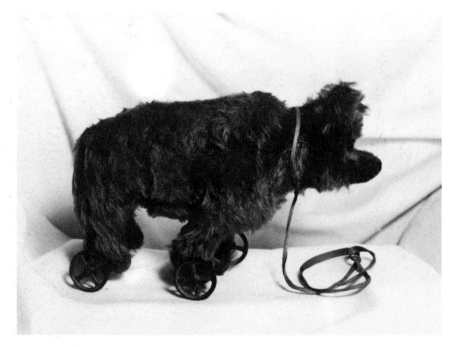

ILLUS. 493. This bear on wheels is 10 1/2in (26.5cm) long, 6 1/2in (16.5cm) tall, made from reddish coloured mohair, glass eyes, excelsior filled, metal chassis and wheels. Thought to be late 1890s. Courtesy L. Albright.

178

JOY TOYS
w o n d e r f u l
range of Soft Toys
now includes Winnie-
the-Pooh, Piglet and
friends, made in Aus-
tralia under ex-
clusive Fran-
chise.

JOY TOYS
have also re-
cently opened new
Showrooms at 255
Broadway, Sydney.
Do come and
see us.

Walt
Disney's film
" Winnie-the-Pooh "
will be released in
Sydney and Mel-
bourne in Aug-
ust.

ILLUS. 494. An advertisement for the Walt Disney Winnie the Pooh made by Joy Toys Pty Ltd in 1967. Courtesy Australasian Sportsgoods and Toy Retailer.

PLUTO   THUMPER   WINNIE THE POOH   BAMBI   VINYL BUILDING BLOCKS
(with Disney characters)
plus a Winnie the Pooh doll

ILLUS. 495 A vinyl Winnie the Pooh made by Metti in the 1960s. Courtesy Metti, S.A.

ILLUS. 496. Two Alpha Farnell Teddy Bears thought to be the same as the one bought from Harrods store in London by A. A. Milne for Christopher Robin. The bear that became Winnie the Pooh. These Teddies are 20in (51cm) tall, and 24in (62cm) tall, soft filled, large glass eyes, thick long mohair coat, shaved muzzle, large paws and a pronounced hump.

ILLUS. 498. The original cardboard tag found on a Schuco YES-NO elephant. Courtesy Pam Hebbs.

YES-NO
A type of Teddy Bear produced by the German company of Schuco (see **Schuco**). By moving the tail a mechanism in the body caused the head to move up and down and sideways.

YOGI BEAR
A popular television character created by Hanna-Barbera. The name was taken from a famous American baseball player Yogi Berra.

A bear that stands on his hind legs and always wears a collar and tie and hat. Yogi Bear has a little friend, Boo Boo. Merrythought of England made a soft toy Yogi from 1961-1964. Made in velvet plush, Yogi stands 11in (27.9cm) tall. A hard plastic Yogi was produced in the 1960s.

YOUNG BULLY
A type of Teddy Bear created by the House of Nisbet (See **Bully Bears**).

ILLUS. 497. Yogi Bear.

ILLUS. 499. A Schuco Yes-No Teddy. 3 1/2in (9cm) tall, fully jointed, mohair fabric with velvet feet. Turned down paw pads, black embroidered nose. This little Teddy has lost the covering of his tail.

ILLUS. 500. A hug of lovable Zotty Teddy Bears. Made by the German firms of Steiff and Hermann. The large Zotty is a 19in (47cm) Steiff, pink with fawn tips with the chest patch, inner mouth and paw pads in peach. He has glass eyes, a velvet muzzle with a brown embroidered nose. He has the turned down front paws of all Zotties. His tip-up growler works very well, emitting a loud growl. In the next row are four Zotties, the two on the left are by Hermann, the two on the right are by Steiff. The Teddy on the extreme left is in mint condition, 9 1/2in (24cm) tall. His mohair coat is brown with white tips, his top lip is embroidered and he has three claws on each paw. His paw pads and inner mouth are pink. The little Hermann next to him is 9in (22cm) tall. His coat is brown with blue tips, he also has his top lip embroidered but has no claws. Both of these Hermann bears have squeakers in their torso. The two little Steiff Zotties are 11in (27cm) and 9in (22cm) tall respectively. They are the same colour, brown, with blonde tips and have a peach coloured chest patch, inner mouth and paw pads. The 11in (27cm) Teddy has claws. The 9in (22cm) has his button in his ear. The little Teddy sitting in the front is 7in (17cm) tall and is also a Steiff. His coat is brown with blonde tips. His chest patch, inner mouth and paw pads are peach in colour. He has three claws on each paw and is fitted with a squeaker. These sometimes underestimated Teddies were all made in the 1960s and 1970s.

Z

ZAKANAKA
A hand-crocheted Teddy Bear created by craftswomen of Botswana as ambassadors.

The word "Zakanaka" means first class. Each Zakanaka Bear has his own official passport.

ZOTTY
A popular style of Teddy made by the German firms of Steiff and Hermann during the 1960s and 1970s.

These cute Teddies are easy to identify and do have several interesting features. The fabric is long-hair mohair with the pile being a different colour from the fabric. Several different coloured Zotty Teddies have been made.

Zotty Teddies have open mouths. The inner mouth is lined with peach coloured felt and is air-brush painted red in the centre. The same colour felt is used on the paw pads. Not all Zotty Teddies have claws, but all do have squeakers.

The front paws are turned down, the muzzle is velvet with the distinctive nose sewn vertically, the outside stitch extending below the line of the rest of the stitches.

A chubby shape make these Teddies look like baby bears.

The Steiff Zotty has a contrasting chest colour.

ZODIAC BEARS
Made by the House of Nisbet Ltd these 14in (36cm) collector's Teddies are a set of twelve dressed to represent the signs of the zodiac.

Capricorn - Dark coloured - wears a dark soft bow and carries a hammer and a telescope.

Aquarius - Dark coloured - wears a peaked soft cap, a large bow tie and carries a handbag.

Pisces - Light coloured - wears a schoolboy's cap, a bow tie, a waist

ILLUS. 501. Two Steiff Zotty Teddy Bears. Fully jointed, 11in (28cm) tall, fawn felt paw pads and inner mouth. Shaved muzzle, glass eyes, button in the ear. Courtesy Marvin Cohen Auctions.

coat and carries a fishing pole.

Aries - Light coloured - wears spectacles, a bow tie, belt and a large watch.

Taurus - Dark coloured - wears a chef's hat marked G B, an apron decorated with a Union Jack, a bow tie and carries a basket of goodies.

Gemini - Light coloured - wears a clown's hat, a reversible ruffled collar and carries a parasol.

Cancer - Light coloured - wears a large bow tie and has a jar of honey.

Leo - Light coloured - wears a large stand-up collar, carries a purse and has a chain belt.

Virgo - White - wears a blue bow, collar and apron.

Libra - Dark coloured - wears a pirate's head scarf, with a gold earring and a fringed neck scarf.

Scorpio - White - wears a boa, a necklace and a decorated soft hat.

Sagittarius - Light coloured - wears a Robin Hood style hat and collar, a belt and a quiver full of arrows.

ILLUS. 502. The twelve Zodiac Bears by House of Nisbet. Courtesy Australasian Sportsgoods and Toy Retailer.

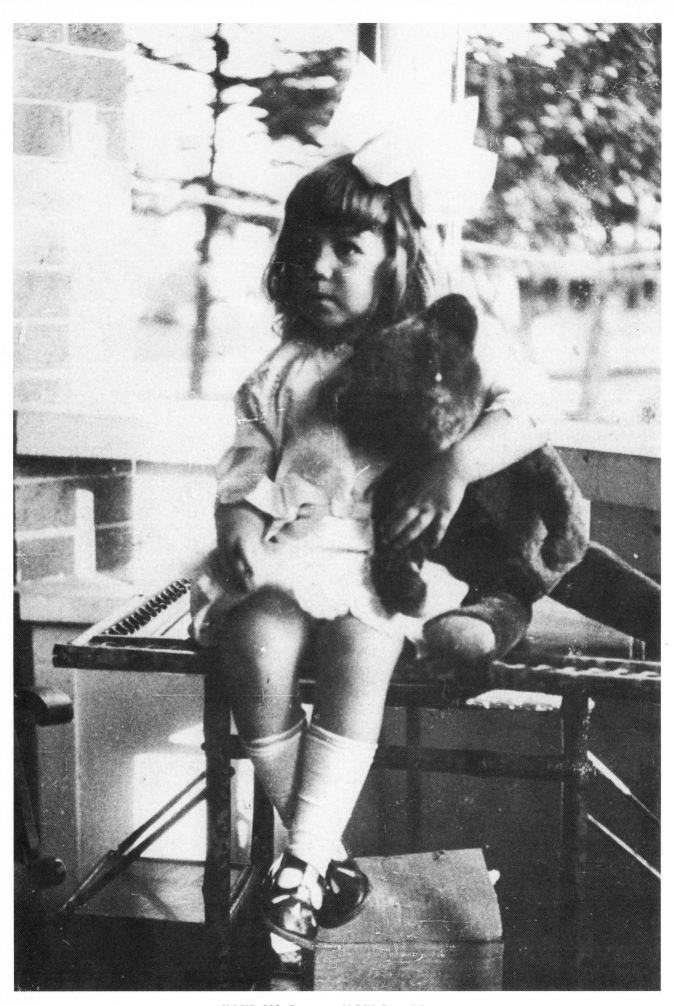

ILLUS. 503. Courtesy N.S.W. State Library.

Bibliography

BOOKS

A Collector's History of the Teddy Bear by Patricia N. Schoonmaker, Maryland, Hobby House Press Inc. 1981.
Bears by Genevieve and Gerard Picot, New York, Harmony Books, 1988.
Button in Ear by Jürgen and Marianne Cieslik, Düsseldorf, Jürgen and Marianne Cieslik Publishers, 1989.
Collectible German Animals Value Guide 1948-1968 by Dee Hockenberry, Maryland, Hobby House Press Inc. 1989.
German Doll Encyclopedia 1800-1939 by Jürgen and Marianne Cieslik, Maryland, Hobby House Press Inc. 1985.
German Toys 1924-1926. Commentary by Dr Manfred Bachmann, Maryland, Hobby House Press Inc. 1985.
Second Teddy Bear and Friends Price Guide by Helen Sieverling, Maryland, Hobby House Press Inc. 1985.
Teddy Bears by Philippa and Peter Waring, London, Treasure Press, 1984.
Teddy Bears and Steiff Animals by Margaret Fox Mandel, Paducah, Collector Books, 1984.
Teddy Bears and Steiff Animals, Second Series by Margaret Fox Mandel, Paducah, Collector Books, 1987.
Teddy Bears on Parade Down Under by Jacki Brooks, Sydney, Australian Doll Digest, 1986.
Teddy Bears Past and Present by Linda Mullins, Maryland, Hobby House Press Inc. 1986.
The Magic of Merrythought by John Axe, Maryland, Hobby House Press Inc. 1986.
The Teddy Bear Men by Linda Mullins, Maryland, Hobby House Press Inc. 1987.
The Teddy Bear and Friends Price Guide by Helen Sieverling, Maryland, Hobby House Press Inc.
Third Teddy Bear and Friends Price Guide by Helen Sieverling, Maryland, Hobby House Press Inc. 1988.

ARTICLES PUBLISHED IN TEDDY BEAR AND FRIENDS®

Teddy Bear and Friends magazine is a registered trademark of Hobby House Press, Inc.

"Poor Misha" by Linda Abbot, Winter 1983/84
"Teddy Bear Christmas Lights" by D. & R. Kubicki, Winter 1983/84
"Jackie, the Jubilee Bear" by Patricia N. Schoonmaker, Spring 1984
"Battery Operated Teddy Bears" by Marty Crisp, Fall 1984
"Teddy Bear Postcards from England" by Rose Wharmsby, Fall 1984
"Berg Teddy Bears" by Evelyn Ackerman, Fall 1984
"1984 is Smokey Bear's Birthday" by Patricia N. Schoonmaker, Fall 1984
"Schuco's Other Miniature Animals" by Evelyn Ackerman, Spring 1985
"Peter Bull's Teddy Bear Collection" by Faith Eaton, Jan/Feb 1986
"There's Magic in Movement" by Evelyn Ackerman, March/April 1986
"Gebr. Hermann - 75th Anniversary Teddy Bear" by Kathy Ann Doll Imports Inc, March/April 1986
"The Zakanaka Bear Story" by Carol -Lynn Rossel Waugh, June 1986
"Discovering Grisly" by Bonnie H. Moore, August 1986
"The Ideal Bear is an American Bear" by Helen Sieverling, August 1986
"Chiltern Teddies and Other Toys Part I" by Patricia N. Schoonmaker, June 1987
"We're Off To See Clemens Spieltiere" by Carol Bond, October 1987
"Who Really Made Those Early Teddy Bears?" by Peter C. Kalinke, October 1987
"History of The Three Bears" by Bernie Crampton, December 1987
"A Bear Called Punkinhead" by Jacqueline Wilson, October 1988
"Meet Robert Raikes" by Rosemary Volpp, April 1989
"Harwin, Maker of Steiff - type Toy Animals in London, 1915 - 1920" by E.J. and D.S. Coleman, October 1989.

INDEX

About The Author

 I have always been a collector of one thing or another, in fact I was a collector when it was called "hoarding junk"!

I collect antique dolls and postcards, Victorian and Edwardian clothes and shoes, antique and early childrens' books, Disney memorabilia, paper dolls, antique baby bowls and miniature china tableware, antique and old dollhouses and miniatures, old dolls' clothes and shoes, Australiana, country furniture, golliwoggs, samplers, old quilts, antique sterling silver and Teddy Bears.

I started to collect Teddies about fifteen years ago when it seemed no-one else wanted them - I could buy a lovely old bear for $5 and something special for $20. I didn't set out to collect Teddies I must admit - they just started to accumulate and voila - a collection. I remember I bought a sweet little Teddy from a fellow dealer who had just purchased it from overseas and I paid the outrageous sum of $65 for it - family, friends and colleagues all predicted a sad end for me. $65 for a worn Teddy Bear! Collecting dolls, postcards and almost everything else had become quite acceptable if not a little eccentric - but to pay good money for a soft toy was somehow the doings of a demented free-spending fool. Today such a different story, now I have so much competition, would seem everyone wants to be an arctophile!!

I am married to a wonderful man who doesn't collect a thing, and while he likes my collections and enjoys my enthusiasm for a new acquisition I know this mania for collecting sometimes mystifies him. When we moved into our first unit after our marriage, I arrived with a truck load of belongings, he with an overnight bag, his engineering books under his arm and his suit slung over his shoulder!

Mike and I have two married children and two little grand-daughters. We are fortunate enough to be able to work from home. We live in a beautiful big old Victorian house set on twenty four acres on the Southern Tablelands of NSW, and we share our home with a few Hereford steers, a small flock of free-range chickens, two cats and our very special friend Sam, a ten year German Shepherd who also loves Teddy Bears.

Mike publishes the AUSTRALIAN DOLL DIGEST and I write for it and am the Editor, we both still deal in antique dolls under the name of Quaint Collectables. Life is full, exciting, sometimes very tiring but never, ever, boring.

Almost three years ago I started to compile this Encyclopedia. I have been so surprised at how much time it has taken. So much re-writing and updating to do, better photos to replace lesser ones, new facts to add to established information.

And so I hope you enjoy this book. It has been a labour of love. I love my Teddy Bears and the added facet that they have added to my life, the people I have met, the friends I have made, the places I have been and all because of Teddies.

The End